THE MEDICAL AND LEGAL ASPECTS OF

SANITARY REFORM

THE VICTORIAN LIBRARY

THE MEDICAL AND LEGAL ASPECTS OF
SANITARY REFORM

ALEXANDER P. STEWART

AND

EDWARD JENKINS

WITH AN INTRODUCTION BY
M. W. FLINN

NEW YORK: HUMANITIES PRESS

LEICESTER UNIVERSITY PRESS

1969

First published in 1866
Second edition 1867
Victorian Library edition (reprinting 1867 text)
published in 1969 by
Leicester University Press

Distributed in North America by
Humanities Press Inc., New York

Introduction copyright © M. W. Flinn 1969

Printed in Great Britain by
Unwin Brothers Limited, Old Woking, Surrey
Introduction set in Monotype Modern Extended 7

SBN 7185 5007 2

THE VICTORIAN LIBRARY

There is a growing demand for the classics of Victorian literature in many fields, in history, in literature, in sociology and economics, in the natural sciences. Hitherto this demand has been met, in the main, from the second-hand market. But the prices of second-hand books are rising sharply, and the supply of them is very uncertain. It is the object of this series, THE VICTORIAN LIBRARY, to make some of these classics available again, at a reasonable cost. Since most of the volumes in it are reprinted photographically from the first edition, or another chosen because it has some special value, an accurate text is ensured. Each work carries a substantial introduction, by a well-known authority on the author or his subject, and a bibliographical note on the text.

The volumes necessarily vary in size. In planning the newly-set pages the designer, Arthur Lockwood, has maintained a consistent style for the principal features. The uniform design of binding and jackets provides for ready recognition of the various books in the series when shelved under different subject classifications.

Recommendation of titles for THE VICTORIAN LIBRARY and of scholars to contribute the Introductions is made by a joint committee of the Board of the University Press and the Victorian Studies Centre of the University of Leicester.

INTRODUCTION

There are two chronologies of public health reform in Victorian Britain: the familiar story of royal commissions and public health acts; and the less well-known progress of the actual state of the health of the general public. The assumption that these two chronologies were closely related is, however, no longer so freely accepted as it used to be. According to the legislative criterion, ten years of reporting and campaigning produced the first real break-through in the Public Health Act of 1848. This, it is commonly assumed, set the reforming ball rolling. The administrative machinery set up by this act of local and central boards of health operating in the general context of "mid-Victorian prosperity" must logically have produced a great improvement in the sanitary state of British towns. The coping-stone of this edifice, coming appropriately at the end of the great Victorian boom – the Public Health Act of 1875 – ensured the completion of this evolution of high standards of public health.

But public health is most simply defined as the elimination of the causes of preventable mortality. In the mid-nineteenth century the mortality that was most easily preventable was that arising from a relatively small group of infectious diseases – typhus, typhoid, cholera, tuberculosis, scarlet and relapsing fever, measles, diarrhoea and smallpox. Public health administration, to be effective, must eliminate, as it virtually has done in mid-twentieth-century Britain, mortality resulting from these diseases. And the plain truth of the matter is that in 1875 the death rate stood at almost exactly the same level as it had in 1838 when civil registration began and Chadwick first sent his poor law medical investigators into the London slums. Infant mortality, the high level of which is commonly assumed to have accounted in large part for the high general mortality level in the early nineteenth century, scarcely began to fall before the end of the century. In short, there was very little real improvement in public

While it would be superfluous in a brief essay of this character to give detailed references, readers of Dr Royston Lambert's Sir John Simon, 1816–1904, *and English Social Administration (1963) will quickly recognise how much this introduction owes to his massive research. This debt is acknowledged here with gratitude.*

health before the last quarter of the nineteenth century; and the most significant reductions to what may be regarded as mid-twentieth-century standards of mortality, including particularly the reductions in infant mortality, were the work of the early twentieth century. The two chronologies – the legislative and the mortality scales – moved forward only with a substantial time-lag between them.

Though, in other words, the 1848 act and the immense labours of Chadwick and others which lay behind it was an essential beginning, the actual achievement in terms of the health of the nation was for a long time negligible. Few of the act's provisions were mandatory, and, in spite of the raucous accusations of the anti-centralisers, the powers of the central board to coerce local authorities were extremely sparingly used. The central board itself was emasculated in 1854 and finally disbanded in 1858. Such local boards as had been created during the brief life of the central board varied widely in their quality. Few had actually appointed Medical Officers of Health, and, even where sewerage schemes were undertaken, they were largely systems for canalising the flow of sewage untreated into the nearest rivers which still, in many cases, remained the sources of supply of drinking water.

Sanitary conditions, however, remained subject to continuing pressures. In spite of emigration, population continued to grow at almost 15 per cent per decade, or at a rate sufficient to double the population in little more than half a century. Since there was little chance of retaining the surplus arising from this natural growth in rural areas, virtually all the growth was necessarily concentrated into the towns. Had these towns been equipped, as they mostly are in the mid-twentieth century, with efficient sewerage and cleansing services and adequate water supplies, their disproportionately fast growth during the third quarter of the nineteenth century would not necessarily have exacerbated the public health problem. But they were not; and to make matters worse there was a persistent move at this period to substitute the water closet for the privies which had formerly constituted the principal means of disposing of domestic sewage. The water closet solved the domestic problem of sewerage, but enormously magnified the public problem. It greatly increased the quantity of liquid sewage, and rendered the old practice of emptying cesspools manually and removing the contents by cart no longer feasible. What was now to happen to this new and rapidly swelling flood of liquid sewage? Even if the sewerage system had been adequate to meet the new requirements, which it seldom was, it remained technically illegal in many places to connect domestic drains to the public sewers. Inadequate and insanitary as the methods adopted in earlier periods had been, the problem facing towns in the middle decades of the nineteenth century was thus temporarily, through the adoption of what may well have been in the long term the most life-saving invention of all time, acutely intensified. Not only were the pre-Chadwickian, square, brick-built sewers quite unfitted to cope with this overwhelming new load, there was as yet no practical solution to the disposal problem beyond discharge, untreated, into rivers.

Thus the public health situation in the 1850s and '60s was one of a haphazard local administration subject to diminishing central guidance attempting half-heartedly to cope with a problem which was intensifying remorselessly.

The collapse of the central board in the 1850s was not, of course, the end of governmental interest in public health. Its functions were transferred to the little known Local Government Act Office[1] and to the newly-created medical department of the Privy Council where a new era of public health administration was inaugurated by the appointment of John Simon as Medical Officer in 1858. Public health legislation, which had been initiated even before the 1848 act,[2] continued almost annually to endow local authorities with essential powers. Much of this legislation attracted little attention at the time so that the Sanitary Commission which reported in 1871 was obliged to observe that "the law is frequently unknown".[3] Little of it finds its way into the textbooks nowadays. Yet in the twenty years after 1848 a score or more acts of considerable importance were passed which, between them, built up a comprehensive, if complex, body of law endowing local authorities in all parts of the country with an immense range of powers.[4] Though, in comparison with the sanitary law of the mid-twentieth century, there were a number of significant aspects of public health still not amply covered by the law up to 1868, most essential powers and functions had been created by then, and it would not be far from the truth to assert that, so comprehensive was the legislation of this period, little more than amendment or codification has been necessary since 1872.

If so much progress was achieved, albeit with ·little publicity,

1 For which see Royston Lambert, "The Local Government Act Office", *Victorian Studies*, VI (1962).
2 e.g. the Vaccination Act, 1846; the Baths and Washhouses Act, 1846; and the Towns Improvements Clauses Act, 1847.
3 *Second Report of the Royal Sanitary Commission, P.P.*, 1871, XXXV, p. 20.
4 The principal acts, which are referred to in greater detail below, were: Nuisances Removal and Diseases Prevention Act, 1848; City of London Sewers Act, 1848; Metropolitan Sewers Act, 1848; Lodging Houses Act, 1850; Common Lodging Houses Act, 1851; Vaccination Act, 1853; General Board of Health Act, 1854; Diseases Prevention Act, 1855; Metropolis Local Management Act, 1855; Nuisances Removal Act, 1855; Local Government Act, 1858; Public Health Acts, 1858 and 1859; Nuisances Removal Act, 1860; Vaccination Act, 1861; Nuisances Removal Act, 1863; Sewage Utilisation Act, 1865; Nuisances Removal Act, 1866; Sanitary Act, 1866; Sewage Utilisation Act, 1867; Sanitary Act, 1868; Local Government Act, 1871; Public Health Act, 1872.

after 1848, why was a second great reform campaign, in which Stewart and Jenkins' masterly pamphlet played a key role, necessary in the late 1860s? The answer to this important question lies in the two basic defects of the mid-Victorian sanitary law – its voluntary nature, and its complexity.

By its very nature, most public health activity must devolve on local government. A decision by Parliament that drainage, cleansing and water supply ought to be undertaken in the interests of the health of the people inevitably therefore raised the issue of the relationship between central and local government; and in the mid-nineteenth century few issues generated so much intense feeling so easily. "In no department of our social economy has the liberty of the subject held more uncontrolled sway than in this death-haunted region of epidemic and infectious disorders."[1] These issues had, perhaps unfortunately, first been raised by the reform of the poor law in 1834. The relief of poverty had been accepted, since the sixteenth century, as a parochial responsibility, and, so far as local administration was concerned, the 1834 act had done no more than enlarge the size of the local authority in substituting unions for individual parishes. But the real novelty of the new administration was the institution of a central authority – the Poor Law Commission – with extensive powers of control over the actions of the local Boards of Guardians; and, with Chadwick as secretary of the new commission, the practice of making this central control a reality was energetically pursued from the start and relaxed little thereafter. Now, while the middle classes in general approved the principles of relief, they showed immediate hostility to the Whitehall interference with functions which had formerly, from at least the mid-seventeenth century, been exercised with very little direction from the centre. With the passage of time, however, the Guardians came to accept the inevitable, and after the transformation of the independent 1834 Commission into the responsible ministry of 1847, poor law administration settled down into routine bureaucracy.

The lesson of 1834 was not lost on the urban middle classes whose local autonomy had, with so little warning, been impaired by the change. After 1834 it was infinitely more difficult for reformers to persuade Parliament to endow central government with any kind of powers over local authorities. In particular, the 1848 Public Health Act severely restricted the powers of the central Board of Health which Chadwick had optimistically hoped would form a counterpart in the sanitary field to his earlier creation for the poor law. But, limited as were the powers of the central Board of Health, with Chadwick and his friends sitting round the table, even these proved too much for the sensitive susceptibilities of the predominant anti-centralizers of the 1850s. The 1848 act, in the event, proved to be the

1 A. P. Stewart, p. 69 below.

trigger which released a violent frenzy of agitation against centralization. It is important to recognise that this was not a simple question
of *laissez-faire* versus state intervention. The issue was not whether
state action ought to be undertaken or not; but *which* authority
should act, local or central government. The anti-centralization
movement, which had first tried its hand with no great success in the
ephemeral anti-New Poor Law demonstrations of 1837–8, burst into
full limelight after 1848 with all the vigour of a brand-new social
philosophy. The campaign owed much to a single individual, the
tireless antiquarian, Joshua Toulmin Smith, founder of the Anti-
Centralization Union. Toulmin Smith's enthusiasm for local government derived from his own rather inadequate researches into the
history of local government which permitted him to present a
highly-idealized version of the local democracies of bygone ages.
By usurping the historic rights of those venerable local bodies, the
central government, in Toulmin Smith's view, was hindering rather
than promoting effective social reform. The spirit of his appeal is
well conveyed in the rather long-winded titles of the pamphlets
which flowed in rapid succession from his pen in the decade after
1848.[1]

For a time Toulmin Smith's over-simplified challenge met the
mood of the period, and social reformers in many fields could only
trim their sails and hope to ride out the storm which swept away,
inter alia, the central Board of Health of 1848, Chadwick and all.
Chadwick's successor in the central administration of public health,
John Simon, who became the first Medical Officer of the reformed
Board of Health in 1855, recognised the need to accept the hostility
to central government coercion as a fact of life, and prepared to plan
his strategy on a general assumption of local autonomy. Within this
stringent limitation, however, his achievements were nonetheless
enormous. With the single exception of vaccination where he felt
that the gains from compulsion were sufficiently indisputable to
justify the use of coercion, he set himself out to rely on persuasion,
publicity, the establishment of a firm scientific base for his department's activities, and the creation of adequate voluntary powers.

1 See, for example, *A Letter to the Metropolitan Sanatory Commissioners: containing
an examination of allegations put forth in support of the proposition for superseding,
in the name of sanatory improvement, all local representative self-government by a
system of centralized patronage* (1848); *Government by Commissions illegal and
pernicious. The nature and effects of all commissions of inquiry and other crown-
appointed commissions. The constitutional principles of taxation and the rights,
duties and importance of local self-government* (1849); *Local Self-Government
un-mystified. A vindication of common sense, human nature, and practical improvement against the manifesto of centralism put forth at the Social Science Association*
(1857) – a reference, seemingly, to the paper by Tom Taylor, "Central and local
action", in *Transactions of the National Association for the Promotion of Social
Science*, 1857, pp. 473–480. His best-known work in this field goes under the
more manageable title of *Centralization or Representation?* (1848).

Coercive powers were limited to the sanctioning of local schemes for the execution of which loans from the Public Works Loan Commissioners were necessary. Otherwise Simon's exiguous staff was used to offer technical advice to local authorities interested enough to solicit it, and in the preparation of reports on special aspects of the problem. The series of reports emanating from the Board, and, after its supersession in 1858, from the Medical Department of the Privy Council, played a valuable role in stimulating both local and central action. Some important items in the legislation of the period 1855 to 1875 originated directly from Simon's office, while, thanks to Simon's quite uninhibited use of of his official status for propaganda purposes, his influence joined with others in contributing more generally to the ultimate improvement of public health law.

The strength of feeling against central government intervention in local affairs in the middle decades of the nineteenth century would probably have been sufficiently great to frustrate any attempt Simon might have made in that direction even had he been minded to follow in Chadwick's footsteps. As a consequence all the legislation after 1848 and up to 1865 at least was permissive in character. It was, as a result, adopted only spasmodically, here and there, and, if this did at least serve to demonstrate the differences between "clean" and "dirty" areas and the effects that could be achieved by the adoption of measures authorised by Parliament, it did little to raise standards generally. In the end Simon began to lose patience, and, from the mid-1860s, he, too, was joining the chorus of reformers asking for powers of compulsion over inactive or obstructive local authorities.

It was too much for even Chadwick to have hoped to create in a single measure a system that would have solved the whole public health problem. The 1848 act was not – and could never have been – the complete answer to the problem. It was a foundation on which a more comprehensive and elaborate structure might subsequently be built. So it was – bit by bit, in a whole series of statutes over the next twenty years, each successive stone in the edifice reflecting new needs, new pressures or new scientific, technological or administrative advances. Each measure, however, was a matter of expediency and acknowledged more the undesirability of rocking the very unstable constitutional boat than an ambition to rationalize the system as a whole. But, sooner or later, a structure built in this way loses the coherence of its initial simplicity. Like the old, overgrown towns with which it was mainly concerned, the piecemeal aggregation of block on block without regard for overall design produced a chaos that in the end demanded reconstruction.

When Chadwick's sanitary enquiry was inaugurated in 1839 it was originally restricted to England and Wales. Believing that some of the worst sanitary conditions were to be found in the working-class housing areas of Glasgow and Edinburgh, Chadwick sought, with success, to have the scope of his enquiry extended to include Scotland. Nevertheless, when it came to drafting the bill which became the Public Health Act of 1848, objections from Scotland, mainly from influential members of the medical profession who questioned the validity of some of Chadwick's basic theoretical assumptions, succeeded in limiting the act to England and Wales. Thereafter, until 1865, none of the sanitary legislation was applied to Scotland: the Sewage Utilisation Act of that year, and the Sanitary Act of the following year both applied to the whole of Great Britain and Ireland. The 1865 act was a curious inroad into a field in which there had hitherto been no official national policy in Scotland, but which was comprehensively tackled in the Public Health Act (Scotland) of 1867 along much simpler lines than south of the border. London, too, had always been treated separately from the rest of the country in the context of public health legislation. And even within the metropolis, the special position of the City had to be safeguarded. Thus, when the first campaign of the 1840s was leading up to the national provision of 1848, the City was dealt with separately from the rest of the metropolis.

The problem of London was only one aspect of the wider administrative question: which authorities were to exercise the necessary powers? When the first bill was being drafted in 1848 there was a range of possibilities. In the towns there were borough corporations, some old but reformed by the 1835 act, and some, as in the big industrial towns, brand new. Many of these towns, as well as most unincorporated towns, were also equipped with bodies of police or improvement commissioners, some of which had demonstrated themselves to be moderately energetic and efficient bodies. In the non-urban areas where the public health problem was generally assumed to be less acute than in the towns, there was a choice between the parish, for long the authority with civil responsibilities, or the more recent, and certainly more efficient, creations of the poor law Guardians. The unpopularity of the New Poor Law was such as effectively to rule out for the time being the possibility of using the latter for the new public health functions. Furthermore, Chadwick had attempted to make the point that a public health authority must control a natural drainage area, and most parishes were too small to qualify in this respect. In the event, therefore, none of the existing authorities were used directly. Local boards of health were specially created for the new role, though in corporate towns it was expected that a committee of the corporation would assume this function. The local boards were conceived initially as operating closely with the new central board, but they were not markedly affected by its disappearance in the 1850s. They continued to function, indeed new ones continued to be created, until replaced by the national network of rural and urban sanitary authorities instituted by the Public Health Act of 1872.

Since public health was conceived initially as an urban problem, the local boards were thought of at first in a civic context, though it was always possible for boards to be set up in rural areas: some, indeed, were. Nonetheless, when it came to the multiplication of rural sanitary powers in the 1850s and 1860s, it was mostly the vestries and the Guardians that were brought into use as authorities. By the mid-1860s, as a result of these piecemeal additions to the sanitary code, almost every existing local authority in town and country had a stake in public health administration.

This confusion would have been bad enough in itself; but it was made infinitely worse by the sub-division of the sanitary law into four different compartments. In the first place there were the public health functions of Local Health Boards (or Local Boards as they were later styled, dropping the word "Health" from their titles) as laid down by the Public Health Act of 1848 and its successors, the Local Government Act of 1858 and the Sanitary Act of 1866. These charged the local authorities who adopted them with basic responsibilities for the public health services of their localities, and empowered them to appoint officials, including Medical Officers, for that purpose. There was, however, secondly, as one of the historical sections of Chadwick's 1842 *Report* showed, a long history of the law, both common and statute, of *nuisances*. The nuisance law was an entity in itself, and statutes for the removal of nuisances, a feature of the statute book since the sixteenth century, continued to be passed through the 1850s and 1860s almost regardless of clashes and overlaps with other departments of the sanitary laws.

"Nuisance" was a vague expression, and one never satisfactorily defined at law. It related, as Chadwick described it, to "anything by which the health or the personal safety, or the conveniences of the subject might be endangered or affected injuriously". For practical purposes it would refer to any offensive refuse in a public or private place; the materials of any noxious industrial process, such as the refuse of slaughterhouses and tanneries, or the smoke or vapours from chemical works; an overflowing privy or cesspool; or a stream or pond used for sewerage purposes. Successive statutes tended to broaden the definition progressively.

Without a comprehensive system of sewers and a reasonably advanced technology of sewage purification and disposal there was bound to be a major problem of nuisance removal, and it is hardly surprising that the mid-nineteenth-century nuisance law was extensive and complex. As the concentration of noxious or offensive trades in towns proceeded and urban population grew, the problem of nuisances was severely intensified. There was something to be said therefore for the Nuisances Removal Acts of 1855, 1860 and 1863 as attempts to stop the gaps of the earlier nuisance law and to provide a comprehensive network of nuisance authorities covering both urban and rural areas. The act of 1855 which first conceived the principle of a national coverage of nuisance authorities groped around for suitable authorities to endow with powers of nuisance removal, and hit, obviously enough, on local boards where they existed, and on vestries elsewhere. The act gave a broad definition of nuisances which included, for the first time, the over-crowding of housing, and made possible the appointment by any nuisance authority of Inspectors of Nuisances. The idea of making use of vestries for these purposes in 1855, however, was not a good one. However efficient they may once have been for local government purposes, for various reasons they had mostly ceased to be so by the 1850s, and it was apparent within a very few years that this attempt to appease the desire for local autonomy had been pushed too far. Very few parishes, in the event, bestirred themselves sufficiently to elect nuisance committees, and fewer still to appoint Inspectors of Nuisances. Accordingly, the Nuisances Removal Act of 1860 substituted Boards of Guardians locally as nuisance authorities in place of vestries. The full range of nuisance powers was retained, and extended by an act of 1863 to include the seizure of diseased food and meat.

From 1855, therefore, it was theoretically possible, subject always to the fact that all the legislation before the mid-1860s was permissive not obligatory on local authorities, for all parts of the kingdom to possess a comprehensive set of powers for the removal of nuisances. But these powers, though embraced in a compact and finite body of law, were grotesquely inadequate. "Even the provisions which regulate the constitution have not universally been found unambiguous", commented Simon.[1] "Boards of Guardians seldom seem aware that the removal of nuisances in country places is entrusted to them."[2] In this respect the nuisance laws of the 1850s and '60s were of a piece with all other branches of the sanitary law. They owed their existence to a desire to fill in the blank spaces between the corporate urban enclaves with authorities competent to deal with the most obvious and urgent problems. It was not initially assumed that there was likely to be a great need for more elaborate and expensive works of the nature of sewerage or water supply schemes in rural areas, so that powers of nuisance removal would be adequate. But reports issued by Simon's department[3] began to make it clear that lack of drainage and clean water could be almost as deadly in the country as in the towns. To meet this particular need, yet another administrative expedient was adopted. The Sewage Utilisation Act of 1865 created

1 *Seventh Annual Report of the Medical Officer of the Privy Council*, P.P., 1865, XXVI, p. 20.
2 *Second Report of the Royal Sanitary Commission*, P.P., 1871, XXXV, p. 21.
3 Particularly the *Sanitary Papers* of 1858. P.P., 1857–8, XXIII.

the new class of "sewer authorities", making it possible for vestries
or improvement commissions to undertake this category of function
hitherto restricted to local boards. It was claimed for this act that
"it introduced into [rural] districts the first real instalment of
active sanitary powers".[1] The act also, as has already been noted, was
the first of the long series of public health acts to apply to the whole
of Great Britain and Ireland, and was amended in the direction of
increasing the powers of the sewer authorities in 1867.

Throughout the whole field of sanitary, nuisance and sewer
legislation there was, from the start, and even more so after 1854,
very little central direction. The powers of Whitehall were largely
confined to the very peripheral function of sanctioning schemes for
which loans were required. In the emergency of a major epidemic,
however, this situation could be transformed. For this was the era
of cholera, and cholera broke through people's constitutional scruples
because it really frightened them. Superimposed, therefore, on the
whole sanitary code was another set of powers in reserve ready to be
swung into action in an emergency which temporarily gave the
central Board of Health or the Privy Council fairly extensive powers
of ordering local preventive works. This body of law was covered by
the Diseases Prevention Acts of 1848 and 1855, dates whose connection
with cholera epidemics is clear enough. The powers – for the speedy
removal of corpses from dwelling houses, the visitation of houses,
and the dispensing of medicines – were valuable enough in themselves, but were not likely to have much real effect on the progress of
a water-borne epidemic like cholera. They did not, for example,
even permit the Board to require local authorities in an epidemic to
cleanse streets, disinfect houses in which cases of diseases had occurred
or to remove nuisances.

As though the complications of these distinct fields of public
health legislation – sanitary, nuisance, sewer, and diseases prevention – were not sufficient, there was, in addition, a whole range of
minor sectors of legislation which served to bring into the public
health field further sets of officials, authorities and central departments. The Burial Acts, for example, of 1850, 1852 and 1853, regulat-
ing the use and location of cemeteries, empowered vestries to appoint
burial boards which could then assume powers granted by the acts.
The Factory Acts from 1833 onwards, and particularly the act
of 1867, attempted to regulate the health conditions of factories and
workplaces, and brought the Board of Trade into the public health
sphere. The 1848 Public Health Act, following the gruesome chapter
in Chadwick's *Sanitary Report* of 1842 on conditions in common
lodging-houses, had already brought this type of housing within
the regulation of local boards. Further special Lodging-House Acts
of 1851 and 1853 strengthened and extended the powers of local

1 *Second Report of the Royal Sanitary Commission, P.P.,* 1871, xxxv, p. 10.

boards in this area. Finally, starting with an act of 1840, there was a series of measures, culminating in a consolidating statute of 1867, dealing with vaccination. This important and highly specialized field was Simon's particular interest. When the code was completed in 1867 it was efficient and workable, but, like all other aspects of public health legislation, excessively complex. Guardians, for example, were required locally to arrange vaccination districts which were to be subject to the approval of the Poor Law Board; but it was the Privy Council which was to make the regulations and arrange for some classes of payments, while the Registrar-General was to supply the forms on which the whole process was controlled. Further on the periphery still, the twenty-year period up to 1868 also saw the creation of codes of law in relation to contagious diseases (the notorious venereal disease legislation), the adulteration of food, pharmacology, alkali works, smoke and quarantine.

While the sheer unwieldiness of this complex of overlapping jurisdictions was not lost on those concerned in its operation in the mid-1860s, its most obvious source of inefficiency, however, still lay in the absence of compulsion. "A great mistake was made", a lawyer stressed to the Sanitary Commission in 1869, "when Parliament receded from the general principle of the Act of 1848 . . ., that people should have no prescriptive right to remain dirty."[1] The requirement that the ratepayers should have the last word was the means whereby, for example, a small town "in a filthy condition" like Biggleswade could steadfastly refuse to undertake the most urgent sanitary works even at the time of an outbreak of cholera.[2] To bring a place under the Public Health or Local Government Acts, a two-thirds majority of the rate-payers was necessary. In default of this improbable concurrence, the place was left to the tenuous prospects of the nuisance laws. "Local self-government, they began to find, meant, on a large and dangerous scale, no government at all."[3]

It was this point, therefore, that reformers, particularly Simon,[4] chose to attack first. The results of their efforts, the important Sanitary Act of 1866 which first seriously introduced compulsory powers, was too hasty to be of lasting importance in the public health field, and, in the event, far from shoring up the top-heavy structure of sanitary administration, proved to be the crowning complexity which finally set in motion the process of reconstruction.[5]

1 *First Report of Royal Sanitary Commission*, *P.P.*, 1868–9, xxxii, Q.4788 (Mr. E. H. Pember). The gloss on the 1848 Act is, perhaps, over-optimistic.
2 *Second Report of Royal Sanitary Commission*, *P.P.*, 1871, xxxv, Q.10,679.
3 Royston Lambert, *Sir John Simon*, p. 355.
4 In the *Seventh Annual Report of the Medical Officer of the Privy Council*, *P.P.*, 1865, xxvi, p. 21.
5 "It reads", commented the *British Medical Journal*, "very much as though its various sections had been printed on separate sheets and shaken in a bag, the sections being then taken out and printed haphazard." (2 March 1867, p. 242.)

The important compulsory powers were formulated in the second and third parts of the act, and were in themselves cumbersome insofar as they added yet another set of authorities both locally and centrally. Part II empowered Chief Constables under the direction of the Secretary of State at the Home Office to take proceedings for the removal of nuisances in default of action by local authorities, while Part III authorised the Secretary of State to undertake neglected works at the expense of a locality if the local authority defaulted and failed to respond to instructions to remedy its omission. Beyond these important provisions, the first part of the act added yet another category to the long list of special functions by permitting vestries to create "special drainage districts" for any part of the area of a parish.

The Sanitary Act was undoubtedly a great step forward, certainly the most significant turning-point since 1848. Simon wrote of "the immense public gain which this recent legislation represents". "The broad effect of this most beneficent legislation", he went on, "may, I believe, be summed up in this simple fact, that influences which have hitherto been causing about a quarter of our total mortality are now for the most part brought within control of the law."[1] Yet within weeks of it being passed an outcry was raised not merely against the flaws in the act itself, but against the anomalies and absurdities of the whole rickety structure – "that enormous mass of insensibility which may be termed Bumbledom", as Edward Jenkins described it.[2] Did the act, he asked in another place, "in an effectual way modify or remove the faults and deficiencies of former legislation? Does it grasp the whole subject in a comprehensive way and propound a scheme which is at once feasible and complete? We think not."[3] Florence Nightingale, who in her dislike of anything connected with Simon was not even prepared to judge by results, condemned the new measure as "a cruel farce" within two months of it receiving the royal assent.[4] Simon himself quickly began to have his reservations about a measure from which he had initially hoped a great deal. The act, clearly, had done nothing to simplify the law: on the contrary, it had added to its complexity. Giving evidence to the Sanitary Commission in 1869 about "the anomalies and perplexities caused by the present jumble of sanitary authorities", Dr H. W. Rumsey observed that "the chaos seems to have been increased by the creation of two classes of sanitary authority by the Sanitary Act of 1866".[5] "Laws which ought to be in the utmost possible degree simple, coherent and intelligible", complained Simon,

1 *Ninth Annual Report of the Medical Officer of the Privy Council*, P.P., 1867, XXXVII, pp. 27–8.
2 *Transactions of the National Association for the Promotion of Social Science*, 1867, p. 545.
3 p. 81 below.   4 Quoted by Royston Lambert, *Sir John Simon*, p. 395.
5 *First Report of the Royal Sanitary Commission*, P.P., 1868–9, XXXII, Q.4294.

"are often, in nearly the utmost possible degree, complex, disjointed and obscure. Authorities and persons wishing to give them effect may often find almost insuperable difficulties in their way; and authorities and persons with contrary disposition can scarcely fail to find excuse or impunity for any amount of malfeasance or evasion."[1] "The state of the law", he said on another occasion, "is chaotic."[2] One aspect of this confusion was exemplified by Rumsey in his evidence to the Commission of 1869:

"How unreasonable is the enactment that, while hospital accommodation is to be provided by the sewer authorities, the carriages which are to convey the sick to those hospitals are to be provided by the nuisance authorities. I admit that a local board may act as both a sewer and a nuisance authority. The sewer authorities are now to provide supplies of medical relief as well as hospital accommodation in the very districts wherein the nuisance authorities, that is the Boards of Guardians, have for the last 35 years had an advanced system of infirmary and medical relief in full operation; and those very boards, that is the Boards of Guardians, under the Disease Prevention Act, may be empowered by the Privy Council to extend this sanitary relief and accommodation during epidemics. Here, then, there are two sets of authorities, which it is well known are in opposition, empowered to do the same work in the same district, each of course ready to throw off the responsibility and to charge the neglect upon the other. The sewer authority may provide hospitals, but it has no staff of medical officers to carry its powers into execution. The nuisance authority has the staff quite ready and daily at work, but it is not empowered to provide the accommodation."[3]

The trouble lay, of course, in the nature of the historical development of the public health system to which the 1866 act was merely the latest increment. The field was, as the Sanitary Commission accepted, "part of a still larger subject, namely, the entire system of local government throughout the country",[4] so that the machinery of sanitary regulation must perforce be designed to operate within the constraints that determined constitutional relationships in the mid-nineteenth century. Though the position achieved by 1875 may have been near to Chadwick's ideal of 1842, in the circumstances of the first half of Victoria's reign the adoption of such a comprehensive system in a single measure was quite beyond the limits of the possible. In default of this, a patient process of aggregation was the only

1 *Eleventh Annual Report of the Medical Officer of the Privy Council, P.P.,* 1868–9, XXXII, p. 22.
2 *First Report of the Royal Sanitary Commission, P.P.,* 1868–9, XXXII, Q.1809.
3 *Ibid.,* Q.4295.
4 *Second Report of the Royal Sanitary Commission, P.P.,* 1871, XXXV, p. 16.

alternative, gaining ground here marginally, and yielding it there
from time to time as local susceptibilities were touched. Such a
piecemeal process could not, of course, produce coherence and logic.
"The number of these statutes", observed the Sanitary Commissioners
in the *Report* of 1871, "and the mode in which they have been framed
render the state of the sanitary laws unusually complex. This complexity has arisen from the progressive and experimental character
of modern sanitary legislation, which has led to the constant enlarge-
ment and extension of existing acts, without any attempt at reconstruction or any regard to arrangement."[1] In all these circumstances, it is hardly surprising that the first recommendation of the
Commission in 1871 was "that it is desirable to make law concerning
public health as simple and uniform as possible."[2]

It was, however, the medical profession which, always in the van
of the movement for public health reform, succeeded in raising
effectively the issue of rationalization. The most vigorous of the
medical reformers was Dr H. W. Rumsey of Cheltenham, and he
shares with Stewart and Jenkins the credit for inaugurating the
campaign for effective revision with a paper on the act of 1866 in
an obscure and ephemeral journal in the autumn of that year.[3] His
paper was subsequently expanded and reprinted in a pamphlet
which later exercised much influence.[4] Dr Alexander P. Stewart,
however, a Glasgow-trained physician practising in London, had
already undertaken a substantial piece of individual research, making
use of a wide network of personal friends and local enthusiasts, into
the extent to which the various local authorities were giving effect
to the sanitary legislation, with particular reference to the appointment and status of medical officers of health and inspectors of
nuisances; and, with the assistance of a legal friend, Edward Jenkins,
he presented his findings to the Manchester meeting of the National
Association for the Promotion of Social Science in October 1866.
The papers were later put together, unaltered, to form the pamphlet
which is now reprinted in this edition.[5]

The choice of the Social Science Association for an audience was
entirely natural. The Association, among whose members public
health reformers from Chadwick and Farr downwards were prominent,
had already ten years of study of social issues, not least of the public
health question, behind it. It had been formed in 1856 on the initiative
of Charles W. Hastings, a reforming barrister whose neglect by the

1 *Second Report of the Royal Sanitary Commission, P.P.*, 1871, XXXV, p. 21.
2 *Ibid.*, p. 174.
3 H. W. Rumsey, "Comments on the Sanitary Act 1866", *Social Science Review*,
  October 1866. Simon credited Rumsey with being "the leading voice" in the
  reform agitation. (*English Sanitary Institutions*, p. 324.)
4 H. W. Rumsey, *On State Medicine in Great Britain and Ireland* (1867).
5 For further details of the original papers and the subsequent pamphlet, see the
  Bibliographical Note which follows this Introduction.

historians of Victorian Britain owes more to the conviction for fraudulent conversion which brought his public career to an end in 1892 at the age of 66 than to any real obscurity of his activities. Under the patronage of Lord Brougham, an extraordinarily distinguished group of public figures interested in social reform was assembled at an inuagural meeting at Brougham's London house in 1856. As well as twenty-seven Members of Parliament and ten Fellows of the Royal Society, its first general committee included Lords John Russell and Shaftesbury, Chadwick and Farr, John Stuart Mill, Kingsley, Ruskin, Kay-Shuttleworth and John Simon. Its meetings took the form of annual conferences held every October in the principal provincial cities. The papers, which ranged over the main problems of mid-Victorian Britain, were printed in annual volumes of *Transactions*. The twenty-nine volumes of this series form an immense, invaluable, and as yet little-used source of Victorian social and administrative history. The Association was truly mid-Victorian in spirit: zealous, enquiring and humane, it was nonetheless conservative in the broad sense of accepting unquestioningly the essential capitalist and constitutional framework of contemporary society. It was no coincidence, therefore, that the emergence of a new temper in the 1880s in the form of more doctrinaire left-wing groups proved the effective death-blow to a body whose personnel was still remarkably unchanged since its formation a generation earlier.[1]

In the 1860s, however, the Association was still an effective pressure group as well as a vigorous forum for social discussion, and its response to Stewart's challenge in 1866 was to take up the cudgels of sanitary reform enthusiastically. In April 1867 a deputation was sent to the Lord President of the Privy Council, the Duke of Marlborough, asking for the consolidation of the sanitary laws, for extension of compulsion, for the improvement and standardization of local health authorities, and for more effective central control.[2] About the same time, and strongly influenced by doctors Rumsey and Stewart, the British Medical Association also joined the fray. In August 1867 the BMA formed a committee on state medicine, and listened to a paper on this subject from Rumsey at its Dublin meeting in the same month.[3] The sanitary laws were again a topic for discussion at the Belfast meeting of the Social Science Association

1 For the history of the Association, see the introduction (pp. xxi–xxxii) by G. W. Hastings to the *Transactions of the National Association for the Promotion of Social Science* for 1857; and B. Rodgers, "The Social Science Association, 1857–1886", *Manchester School*, xx (1952), 283–310.

2 The deputation, which was led by Sir James Kay-Shuttleworth, included Rumsey and Stewart. (*British Medical Journal*, 13 April 1867, p. 431.) Its memorial and the speeches with which it was presented on this occasion are printed as an appendix to Stewart and Jenkins, *The Medical and Legal Aspects of Sanitary Reform*, pp. 96–100.

3 *British Medical Journal*, 7 September 1867.

in October, when Mr W. H. Michael, a barrister, led a discussion on "What measures are necessary to secure efficiency and uniformity in the working of the sanitary laws throughout the kingdom ?"[1]

The two associations, linked by common members like Stewart and Rumsey, quickly came round to the view that what was needed was a royal commission. Joint action between the two associations was suggested during the discussion following Rumsey's paper to the BMA at Dublin, and, on the proposal of the veteran leader of public health reform, Dr William Farr of the Registrar-General's office, a joint committee of the two associations was formed early in 1868 with Edwin Chadwick as its chairman. The BMA's nominees for the joint committee included Rumsey and Stewart among a distinguished group of active medical reformers.

When it came to the details of what the two associations should jointly recommend for future policy there was naturally some debate, and it was not until May 1868 that the joint committee was able to agree on the details of a memorandum which had initially been put together by Rumsey. While setting out the respects in which the committee felt that the law needed to be amended, the memorandum was primarily concerned to ask for "a thorough, impartial, and comprehensive inquiry into the operation of the several laws, regulations, and customs, under which members of the medical profession are employed, constantly or occasionally, in the towns and rural parishes of England, Scotland and Ireland, or in some of them – by different departments of government, by public bodies, by local authorities, or in voluntary societies".[2] Later the same month the Lord President of the Council received a deputation from the two associations bearing their memorandum.[3] This pressure was successful, and in November 1868 the Royal Sanitary Commission was appointed with a wide remit to consider the whole state of the sanitary laws.[4] The collapse of the Conservative government, however, immediately afterwards, led to the supersession of the commission, but it was re-appointed early in 1869 shortly after the formation of the new Liberal ministry. Although the revised commission omitted some of the reformers like Rumsey, Hastings and Stewart who had been

1 *Transactions of the National Association for the Promotion of Social Science,* 1867, pp. 462–4, 541–8.
2 *British Medical Journal,* 23 May 1868, p. 513.
3 The speeches prepared for this occasion are printed in the *British Medical Journal,* 30 May 1868, pp. 541–3. Among the members of the deputation were Rumsey, Chadwick, Farr, Hastings (General Secretary of the Social Science Association), Guy, Stewart and Jenkins—a memorable group of sanitary reformers.
4 J. A. Symonds, in an "Address on health" to the Bristol meeting of the Social Science Association in 1869, attributed the appointment of the Commission to the work of Rumsey, Acland, Farr, Stewart, Clode and Michael. (Dr Acland was President of the British Medical Council, and Mr Clode a member of the staff of the General Register Office. Michael, like Jenkins, was a barrister.)

named on the original commission, it included among its twenty-one members no less than nine members of the Social Science Association. The way was now opened to a thoroughgoing reconsideration of the whole structure of public health administration.

The Commission reported in 1871, embodying its recommendations in the form of a draft statute. It led, therefore, directly to the Local Government Act of 1871 and the Public Health Act of 1872 which respectively revised the structure of central and local administrations of public health.[1] In greater leisure the whole corpus of laws was finally consolidated and codified in the great Public Health Act of 1875. Though the act of 1875 marked the culmination of a long process of improvement in the sanitary laws, so far as the health of the people was concerned, the achievement of a rationalized and codified sanitary law in 1875 only marked the beginning of the fall in mortality. In spite of the important work that had been done randomly in many of the major concentrations of population during the previous quarter-century under the authority of a multitude of local private acts as well as of all the national legislation reviewed in this intro-duction, advances on the broad front of the whole country were only finally made possible by the reform campaign from 1866 to 1875.

The success of this campaign was the achievement almost entirely of members of the medical profession both within and without the public service. In this circumstance it is hardly surprising that the agitation was directed primarily with an eye to the role of doctors in the state system. Doctors were extensively employed by central and local authorities in mid-Victorian Britain, and as they began in the middle decades of the century to acquire a corporate voice and confidence they naturally sought to enhance their role and raise their status in the public service. Rumsey's efforts were directed quite unequivocally to this end, and Stewart's major share in his joint work with Jenkins is simply a broader approach to the same goal. Stewart's desire to promote the status of doctors sprang from his conviction of their real worth in reducing mortality. What bothered him were the frustrations of lack of powers, of the ignoring of doctors by the very authorities that employed them, and of under-utilization of their services in situations crying out for intensive action. Derisory payment he took as merely a symptom of the sheer lack of interest of local authorities in the health of the people. Thus the main objects of Stewart's attack were the local authorities, though his irritation with "the *inertia* of the Privy Council"[2] indicates that he was also anxious to strengthen and revitalize the central authority. Nonethe-less he accepted the view that the role of government was simply to create conditions within which local reformers could overcome the

1 There were, of course, respects in which the statutes did not exactly follow the recommendations of the Commission.
2 p. 23 below.

opposition of inert or hostile local majorities of rate-payers. Stewart's extensive local researches into the employment and remuneration of doctors and other health officials were aptly wedded to Jenkins' revelation of the confusion of authorities. The joint work convinces by the sheer weight of telling fact as well as by the vigour of the argument. With the additional virtues of conciseness and readability, the pamphlet was both an effective piece of propaganda and a useful research document. Though it deserves to be read from both points of view today, its joint authorship nonetheless effectively illustrates the dual aims of the reformers, a division which might easily have turned to their disadvantage. The concern of the medical profession for its own position in a system of "state medicine" was natural enough, though it ran the risk of being interpreted as self-interest; but it was far less ambitious than the broader aim of disentangling the administrative chaos, the goal pursued by the lawyers and administrators who predominated in the Social Science Association. And since Stewart's share in the joint work with Jenkins was the lion's one, the impact of its publication on the general public may well have been the less in consequence.

The pamphlet was nevertheless a key document in the whole process of sanitary reform which unfolded from 1866 to 1875, though its contribution to final success is more likely to have been indirect than direct. The reforms themselves derived more obviously from the lobbying of the Medical and Social Science Associations: since these were large bodies, each embracing a fairly wide diversity of opinion, it may not be unreasonable to see papers such as those by Stewart and Jenkins as being primarily concerned with the conversion of the lobbying bodies themselves, rather than as influences on a wider, public opinion. There are many phases of any reform movement and the preliminary ones are no less vital than the final ones.

M. W. Flinn

BIBLIOGRAPHICAL NOTE

The present volume reprints the pamphlet published in 1867 by Robert Hardwicke of London under the title *The Medical and Legal Aspects of Sanitary Reform*. A note on the verso of the title-page states that the two papers included in the pamphlet "were in substance brought before the Social Science Congress at Manchester, in October, 1866".

Alexander P. Stewart's paper, entitled in the pamphlet "The Medical Aspects of Sanitary Reform", was first published in *Transactions of the National Association for the Promotion of Social Science*, 1866, pp. 494–569. Its title in the *Transactions* was "On the Results of Permissive Sanitary Legislation; or, the Medical Aspects of the Laws relating to the Public Health" and the article had the headline "The Medical Aspects of Sanitary Legislation". The 1867 pamphlet appears to reprint the essay from the type used in the *Transactions* but there are variations in distribution on pp. 15–16 and 75–77. Throughout the 1867 text footnote references to *Soc. Sc. Transactions* replace the simple reference to *Transactions* which sufficed in the original printing. The first footnote on p. 43 and the list of "Sanitary Queries" on pp. 78–79 are additions.

Edward Jenkins' paper was first published in *Transactions of the National Association for the Promotion of Social Science*, 1866, pp. 478–494, under the title "The Legal Aspect of Sanitary Reform" with the headline "Sanitary Law Reform". In the 1867 pamphlet the title is changed to "The Legal Aspects of Sanitary Reform". Again the essay appears to have been reprinted from the type used in the *Transactions*.

The account of the Association's deputation to the Duke of Marlborough on pp. 96–100 of the 1867 pamphlet is an addition.

J. L. Madden

THE

MEDICAL AND LEGAL ASPECTS

OF

SANITARY REFORM.

BY

ALEXANDER P. STEWART, M.D.,

AND

EDWARD JENKINS,

BARRISTER-AT-LAW.

LONDON:
ROBERT HARDWICKE, 192, PICCADILLY.
1867.

—

Price Half-a-Crown.

The following Papers were in substance brought before the Social Science Congress at Manchester, in October, 1866.

THE

MEDICAL ASPECTS OF SANITARY REFORM.

THERE are special seasons in our history—whether personal, national, or social—which invite us to pause, and look backward as well as forward; to reckon up the gains and losses, the wise and the false moves of the past; and, by the light of experience, both past and present, to forecast and lay plans for the future. Such a season in our sanitary history is the present. The Lord President of the Council stated to a deputation that waited upon him in the month of July, for the purpose of urging, among other things, the consolidation of our sanitary laws, that the late government thought it better, after mature deliberation, to defer the work of consolidation till next session, when it would probably occupy the attention of Parliament. The consolidation of a number of statutes is very much like the stereotyping of a book, giving permanence and the stamp of authority to all uncorrected errors, which often pass from mouth to mouth as accepted and recognised truths, till some voice from the grave, in the shape of a posthumous diary or correspondence, proclaims their falsehood to another generation of readers. My object, therefore, in this paper is to inquire briefly what have been the substantial results of our sanitary legislation, what great principles have been embodied in it, and accepted, at least in theory, by the community at large; and what, looking forward to the consolidation of our health laws, are the mistakes to be corrected, and the objects to be not only desired but striven for by all who take an interest in the health of the people. It is not that I have much that is new to say on a nearly threadbare subject, or that I can hope, in my mode of saying it, to emulate my betters, who have spoken and written so well upon the public health from time to time during the last twenty years. But I have thought it possible that a new voice speaking on an old and hackneyed topic might arrest some whom the familiar accents of old acquaintances had failed to impress, and stir to action ; and encourage the veteran labourers in this good cause by the assurance that there are others who not only wish them " God speed," but are anxious to lend them a helping hand. And with the view of eliciting a thorough discussion of this vital question, my friend Mr. Edward Jenkins and I have arranged that I should present the medical, and he the legal, aspects of our sanitary laws.

The laws of health, and the disastrous results of disregarding or transgressing them, though comparatively new to the public, have long been a subject of deep interest to the profession to which I have the honour to belong. Here is a striking and instructive passage, published rather more than a hundred years ago by a great master in the art of healing:—" From this view of the causes of malignant fevers and fluxes, it is easy to conceive how incident they must be, not only to all marshy countries after hot seasons, but to all populous cities, low and ill-aired, unprovided with common sewers, or where the streets are narrow and foul, or the houses dirty; where fresh water is scarce ; where jails and hospitals are crowded and not ventilated, or kept clean ; where, in sickly times, the burials are within the walls, and the bodies not laid deep ; where slaughter-houses are likewise within the walls, or where dead animals and offal are left to rot in the kennels or on dunghills; where drains are not provided to carry off any large body of stagnating or corrupted water in the neighbourhood; where flesh meats make the greatest part of the diet, without a proper mixture of bread, greens, wine, or other fermented liquors; where the grain is old and mouldy, or has been damaged by a wet season, or where the fibres are relaxed by immoderate warm bathing. I say, in proportion to the number of these or the like causes concurring, a city will be more or less subject to pestilential diseases, or to receive the leaven of a true plague when brought into it by merchandise," *—a passage which exhibits well the noblest aspect of medicine, making earnest, though often thankless and unheeded efforts for the prevention of disease.

Seventy years passed away, and a visitation of pestilence came, before the principles thus clearly and decisively set forth by Sir John Pringle in the middle of last century began to awaken the attention of the public. And such was the effect of the epidemic of 1832 that, though the spasmodic and almost frantic efforts made by the panic-stricken populations ceased with the departure of the unwelcome visitant, the impression made on not a few thoughtful minds, by the sickening glimpses they had had of " the lowest deep " of British society, could not be effaced, and prompted them to enter upon a life-long career of active beneficence that has already conferred lasting benefits upon the entire community. In some places, as in Exeter, the history of which during the visitation of the cholera has been graphically and impressively written by Dr. Shapter, the immediate result was a great improvement in the sanitary arrange-

---

* Pringle's " Observations on the Diseases of the Army," 6th edition. London, 1768 ; p. 324.

ments of the city, especially as regards water supply. It was then that the era of sanitary legislation commenced, thus affording a striking illustration of the truth of Hecker's remark, " that great epidemics are epochs of development, wherein the mental energies of mankind are exerted in every direction." We have reason to be thankful that during the last thirty years there has been a large and steady increase in the numbers of our sanitary reformers. Few in comparison with the great mass of the nation, but still in themselves a host, there are scattered over the face of the counties, and congregated in considerable numbers in our large cities, men of broad and enlightened views, who thoroughly comprehend the close and reciprocal relations that subsist between dirt, disease, drunkenness, pauperism, and crime, and who have long done their utmost to promote the adoption in their respective neighbourhoods of right sanitary opinions and effective sanitary measures. And the result is seen in the great and growing attention accorded by the legislature to all questions bearing upon the public health.

Parliament has not neglected its duty in this matter. While I concur in the feeling now becoming very wide-spread, that the tone of our sanitary legislation has of late years been rather timid and apologetic, I maintain that Parliament has been, till lately, far in advance of the national sentiment on matters relating to the public health. Let us glance at what has been done since 1832. Beginning in the following year, with the case of the factory children, as if to intimate that the Imperial Parliament would succour and relieve the oppressed at home as well as in the West India colonies, they prohibited, in 1834, the cruel and murderous practice of employing climbing boys for sweeping chimneys ; in 1840 and 1841 they passed the Act to extend the practice of vaccination ; and in 1842 they declared illegal the employment of women and children in mines and collieries, the horrors connected with which inhuman system were exhibited by the noble author of the measure† in terms of indignant eloquence, which awoke a responsive echo in every corner of the realm. About this time appeared that remarkable series of volumes‡ on the sanitary condition of the labouring classes, for which we were indebted chiefly to Mr. Chadwick, and which, revealing as they did an almost incredible state of matters in our crowded centres of population, were read by multitudes with a strange and eager interest, and formed the basis of our subsequent legislative enactments. The first attempts to obtain the assent of the legislature to the recommendations of the Health of Towns Commissioners, were the Town and House Drainage Bills of Lords Lincoln and Normanby, and the Health of Towns Bill introduced by Lord Morpeth, in 1845. These attempts, though unsuccessful, contributed, not less by the

* Hecker's " Epidemics of the Middle Ages;" Sydenham Society's Translation, p. 177.
† Lord Ashley.
‡ " General Local Reports on The Sanitary Condition of the Labouring Population of Great Britain," July, 1842.

opposition than by the attention and sympathy which they awakened, to the success of similar measures in after years.

Then followed, in rapid succession, the Acts for Promoting the Establishment of Baths and Washhouses, both in Great Britain and Ireland, in 1846; the Towns' Improvement Act in 1847; the Public Health, the Nuisances' Removal, and the City of London Sewers'* Acts in 1848; the Metropolitan Interments Act in 1850, followed in 1853 by a similar Act for the whole of England,† the Act to Encourage the Establishment of Lodging Houses for the Labouring Classes,‡ and the Common Lodging Houses' Act in 1851; the Metropolitan Water Act in 1852; the Smoke Nuisance Abatement (Metropolis) Act, and the Act to Extend and make Compulsory the Practice of Vaccination, in 1853; the Merchant Shipping Act, with its stringent provisions for the preservation of the health of our merchant seamen, in 1854; the Diseases Prevention, the Metropolis Local Management, the Metropolitan Buildings, and the Nuisances' Removal Amendment Acts, in 1855; and the Public Health Act, 1858, which abolished the General Board of Health, and vested its powers in the Privy Council. Since then there have been added to the statute book the Acts for the purification of the Thames in 1858 and 1866; the Nuisances' Removal Amendment Act in 1860; the Act for preventing the Adulteration of Articles of Food and Drink in the same year; the Acts (passed in 1860, 1861, and 1864) which included under the provisions of the Factory Acts women and children employed in bleaching and dyeing works, in lace factories, and in the manufacture of earthenware, of lucifer matches, of percussion caps and cartridges, of paper staining and of fustian-cutting ;§ the Vaccination Amendment Act in 1861; the Act for the Seizure of Diseased and Unwholesome Meat, and the Alkali Works Act, in 1863; the Sewage Utilization Act in 1865; the Labouring Classes' Dwelling Houses Act, and the Sanitary Act, in 1866.

Let us attempt to condense into a few sentences the great principles embodied in this vast mass of legislation. They are as follows :— That the employment of women and children in laborious occupations for which they are physically unfit, is physiologically as well as politically and morally wrong; that the sanitary state of our large towns, and the condition, physical as well as moral, of our labouring population, are matters of imperial interest, which we cannot with impunity neglect; that various diseases, which prevail among us, either epidemically or endemically, and are attended with a high

---

* In section 91 of this Act is the only definition of a common lodging-house, which existed for many years. The common lodging-house Acts contain none!
† Between 1850 and 1861, not fewer than *eight* Burial Acts passed through Parliament.
‡ Very little use has been made of this admirable measure.
§ See " Extension of the Factory Acts." By H. S. Tremenheere. *Soc. Sc. Transactions* 1865; pp. 291-294.

mortality, depend wholly or in part on neglect of the laws of health and disregard of the common decencies of life, and are in great measure preventible by a few simple precautionary measures; that a sufficient supply of pure air and water is essential to health, and therefore, that the overcrowding of workshops, dwellings, and schools, the contamination of the air by smoke or other irritating foreign particles, by noxious gases, the product of organic decomposition, and by chemical fumes, and the pollution of water by sewage and other refuse should, as fruitful sources of disease, be prevented; that the establishment of baths and washhouses, and the erection of suitable dwellings for the labouring classes should be encouraged; that efficient drainage should everywhere be promoted, but that the conversion of streams and rivers into common sewers is a monstrous perversion of the gifts of Providence and a great public wrong ; that the practices of conveying persons smitten with contagious or infectious disorders in hackney carriages, and of retaining the decomposing remains of the dead in the crowded abodes of the living, are full of peril, and therefore to be discouraged; that with the view of discovering and removing such evils as affect directly or indirectly the health of the community, medical officers of health and inspectors of nuisances are needed, the latter not to wink at the continuance of nuisances, but to ferret them out and drag them to the daylight, the former to report from time to time the results of inspection and inquiry to the proper authorities, with such suggestions as may seem to him best fitted to remedy existing abuses; that it is the duty of local authorities to take cognizance of and remove all nuisances and impediments to the public health, and to promote such measures as may be conducive thereto ; that, in the event of the local authority declining to act, any inhabitant of any parish or place may complain to a magistrate, who shall proceed as if he were the local authority, with a view to the abatement of the nuisance complained of; and finally, that, in the event of a local authority making default in providing its district with sufficient sewers or water supply, complaint may be made to a Secretary of State, who shall inquire and proceed in the matter as he may see fit; in other words, that every facility shall be given to the inhabitants for compelling the local authority to perform its duty. Let us note in addition, that since 1858, we have had in the Privy Council a Public Health Department, which presents us annually with a volume full of interesting and important material, and exercises a summary jurisdiction in times of epidemic visitation.

When I have said that for the authoritative recognition and sanction of all these principles, so pregnant with potential benefits, we are indebted to the legislature, I have surely said enough to defend it from those, and they are many, who would lay upon its shoulders the chief blame of our sanitary deficiencies. It is a matter of great moment to have the stamp of legislative approval affixed to the great principles and doctrines for which sanitary reformers have long contended; and if the country had taken the thirty or forty times repeated hints offered them by Parliament, how very different would our sanitary condition have been at this good hour! But when I have said this, I have said all that is due to the Parliaments and Governments of the last thirty-five years. Somehow or other we are apt to look to our law-givers not for hints, but for laws. If the principles recognized and sanctioned by them are thoroughly sound, we have a right to expect that, if not at first, they will sooner or later carry them out to their logical consequences—*i. e.*, enforce them. Of all the Acts I have recited, five only, so far as I know, can boast of a complete or fair measure of success. The Factory Acts are, I believe, thoroughly effective ; women and children are no longer employed in mines and collieries ; intramural burials are a thing of the past ; the Metropolis Water Act has doubtless saved a multitude of lives ; and the sanitary organization of the Metropolis approaches more nearly to the ideal of sanitary reformers, than that of any other large town in the kingdom. In all of these cases the legislature has not only had the courage to say " you shall," instead of " you may," but has made obedience to its injunctions a necessity. On the other hand, the Chimney Sweepers' Acts, * the Smoke Nuisance Acts, the Vaccination Acts, and the Merchant-shipping Act, as regards the prevention of scurvy, † though penal in their provisions, are all more or less failures for want of being duly enforced; and, as we all know, the Sanitary Acts proper are in great measure a failure. Why ? Simply because they are suggestions rather than laws. So much is this the case, that, as Mr. Rumsey points out in a very able paper published in this months' (October, 1866) *Journal of Social Science*, the Local Government Act has been adopted by many small places, with the express intention of evading the Highway Acts, and without any intention of carrying out the other. And Mr. Simon, in his Eighth Report, lately published, § narrates the case of several parishes in the Malling Union, which were infested with typhus and diphtheria, and threatened with cholera, were drinking polluted water and overspread with all sorts of nuisances, but could not obtain the improvements which they earnestly desired on account of the dogged obstructiveness of the Board of Guardians, who successfully bearded the Health Department of the Privy Council, Sir George Grey, and the law-officers of the Crown, declaring that " they did not consider the 5th Section of 23 & 24 Vict., c. 77, to be imperative, and they therefore declined to appoint a committee under it." So much for permissive legislation! Let us glance at some of its other developments.

The basis of all effective local operations in health matters must be full, accurate, and trustworthy information. This may be procured in various ways, and from various sources. It may be sought for and

---

* *Soc. Sc. Transactions*, 1864, p. 591.
† "On the Health of Merchant Seamen." By J. O. McWilliam, M.D., *Soc. Sc. Transactions*, 1861, p. 509; also *Soc. Sc. Transactions*, 1862, p. 544; and " Report of the Liverpool Committee on the ' Health of Merchant Seamen.'" By Rev. S. A. Steinthal, p. 555.
§ Eighth Report of the Medical Officer of the Privy Council, pp. 23-25.

made known by local authorities, by local associations, or by public spirited individuals, or failing any or all of these, by the Health Department of the Privy Council. Throughout our sanitary laws—which we cannot yet properly call a system or code—three things are tacitly assumed, viz., 1. That to the local authority (the meaning of which very complex term will be explained by Mr. Jenkins,) belongs the duty of caring for the health of its constituents. 2. That the local authority will neglect that duty, and 3. That the local authority must not be expressly enjoined to do its duty. Of these three postulates, it is hard to say which is the more essential to the right understanding of our subject. One thing is very clear, that Parliament, which at first prescribed no remedy for the obstructiveness of local authorities, has of late years found it necessary, in each successive Act, to arm the individual householder or inhabitant with more extensive powers, till, in the Sanitary Act of 1866, it is provided that a single complainant may call a recusant corporation to account for its default before one of Her Majesty's principal Secretaries of State. In this way, and also by empowering the Privy Council * to institute sanitary inquiries and report the results thereof annually to Parliament, the legislature, with a becoming jealousy of anything like undue interference with local self-government, has long been endeavouring to create a public opinion in favour of sanitary reform, and so to direct it as to overcome the sluggishness and prejudice of niggardly and self-complacent "bumbledom" both in town and country. Some places, as, for instance, Liverpool and Leicester, have for many years enjoyed the services of able, energetic, and judicious medical officers of health ; and other towns—such as Birkenhead, Bristol, Doncaster, Dundee, Edinburgh, Glasgow and Leeds—have more recently recognized the necessity of appointing such officers, with active and intelligent sanitary detectives under them, and have shown themselves ready to lend a hearty support to their officials in the discharge of their disagreeable and arduous duties. But if they be otherwise minded—and we shall presently see how often they are so—the law, beyond the limits of the Metropolis, while suggesting the propriety of appointing, acquiesces in the non-appointment of medical officers of health ; and since 1860, the injunction of the Nuisances' Removal Act, 1855, to appoint inspectors of nuisances, has actually been withdrawn !

Before inquiring what has been done by public bodies, let me mention a few of the contributions which individual or private effort has made to our sanitary knowledge. Before 1849, the late Dr. Snow was conspicuous for his advocacy of the opinion that cholera is propagated by the use of pump-water, which in large towns is usually contaminated by surface drainage. The eager pertinacity with which he urged his views, in season and out of season, was amusing to some and irksome to many. But after the memorable and very fatal out-

---

* Public Health (Privy Council) Act, 1858, secs. 5 and 6.

break of the disease in Albion Terrace, Wandsworth*—a genteel row of detached houses occupied by professional men and tradespeople— his reasonings found more patient and respectful listeners. Not that the evidence in favour of his theory was perfectly conclusive — for, though the spring which supplied these houses with water was polluted by the bursting of the drain common to all of them, another hypothesis referred the outbreak to the removal, from the house where the first death occurred, of a heap of horribly offensive rubbish which had been slowly accumulating for two years. But though the probabilities, as between air and water, were thus pretty evenly balanced, the idea that Dr. Snow's views might possibly be true was firmly fixed in the public mind, and many who, like myself, could not admit their being proved, were tacitly of opinion that they were highly probable. That there was some connexion, more or less intimate, between the water supply of towns and the spread of cholera, was further forced on the minds of many by Dr. Shapter's statements regarding Exeter in 1832, then one of the cities worst supplied with water and most severely visited, and the same city in 1849, when its water-supply was admirable, and it was almost exempt from the disease. The same immunity was observed in various towns, e. g. Bath, Birmingham, Cheltenham, and Leicester, which " were supplied with water quite uncontaminated with the contents of sewers." These and other circumstances combined to give weight to Dr. Snow's conclusion, that " the sanitary measure most required in the Metropolis is a supply of water for the South and East districts of it, from some source quite removed from the sewers."

The results of his laborious investigations into the connexion between the water-supply and the death-rate from cholera in the various districts of London, were made public in November and December 1851.† It appeared that the cholera was very much more severe on the south side of the Thames than on the north. The water of the Chelsea Company, though taken from the Thames at Chelsea, where it was very foul, was much purer than that of the Lambeth, Vauxhall and Southwark Companies, because, having till a short time previously had "to supply the Court and a great part of the nobility, they had large and expensive filters, and also very capacious settling reservoirs, in which the water is kept for a considerable time before its distribution;" whereas the other companies filtered the water supplied by them very imperfectly through coarse gravel, and allowed no time for subsidence. The mortality in those districts supplied by the Chelsea Company, though great, was considerably less than in those supplied by the other companies. The General Board of Health, in their report presented to Parliament in 1850, select, "out of great numbers" from all parts of the kingdom, the outbreak of diarrhœa in Hackney, and of cholera in Windmill Square, Shoreditch ; in

---

* *Medical Gazette*, new Series, Vol. ix.; 1849. pp. 468 to 504; also, Snow on Cholera, 2nd edition; 1855, pp. 25-30.
† "Report on the Epidemic Cholera in 1848 and 1849," pp. 59-62.

Rotherhithe ; in Horsleydown ; in Waterloo Road, Lambeth ; and in Hope Street, Salford, as "proving the influence of the use of impure water in predisposing to the disease."

The subject was at length brought before Parliament, and a law enacted, as we have seen, in 1852, compelling the water companies to make arrangements for conveying the water from above Teddington lock. Already in 1853 the death-rate from cholera in the district supplied by the Lambeth Company, which alone had completed its works and brought its supply from Thames Ditton, was little more than one-half the Southwark and Vauxhall death-rate. The house to house inquiry undertaken by Dr. Snow in the Lambeth, Vauxhall, and Southwark districts in the autumn of 1854,[*] brought to light the startling fact, that out of a total of 1,510 deaths, 1,224 occurred in houses supplied by the Southwark and Vauxhall, and only 93 in those supplied by the Lambeth Company. In other words, " while a death from cholera had occurred in one house in every 28 supplied by the Southwark and Vauxhall Company, a fatal attack of cholera had occurred in only one out of 251 houses supplied by the Lambeth Company," showing a mortality "just nine times as great in the houses supplied by the former company as in those supplied by the latter." And now it was found that the death-rate in the Chelsea district, which had previously presented so favourable a contrast to that of the southern districts, was very large when compared with the Lambeth rate. In short, it was very clear that the extraordinary diminution of the mortality in a district abounding in unwholesome influences, and hemmed in on every side by districts ravaged by cholera, from which it had itself suffered frightfully in 1849, had more than a casual connection with the pure water supplied by the Lambeth alone of all the water companies. Even more striking was the immunity enjoyed by single tenements supplied by this company, while all around the pestilence was busy and terribly fatal. The evidence collected in the same year (1854) by this indefatigable inquirer as to the origin of the frightful outbreak in the Golden Square district in the month of September, was such as to compel the assent of the most incredulous to the proposition that it was mainly attributable to the contamination of the water of the Broad Street pump-well, the favourite source of supply in that neighbourhood. What was then matter of doubt, or wonder, or disgust to multitudes, now forms an almost unchallenged article in our sanitary creed, of which the Metropolis Water Act was one of the earliest expressions, as the yearly growing interest in the question of water supply for our great towns is its natural and gratifying result.

But while thankfully acknowledging our obligations to Dr. Snow, who spent much time, and strength, and substance, in conducting this great inquiry, I cannot admit that cholera spreads only by being swallowed. That the gaseous emanations from unremoved cholera

---

[*] *Medical Times and Gazette*, New Series, vol. ix., pp. 365-6,1854.

discharges in privies, mines, etc., are a very frequent cause of the extension of the disease, seems to me established beyond dispute by the facts stated in a series of letters * from the pen of that accomplished and sagacious physician, Dr. W. Budd, of Bristol, who has established as strong a case for prompt measures of isolation and disinfection as has Dr. Snow for an abundant supply of pure water. This is not the fitting place for discussing the question whether water contaminated by ordinary sewage may, under varying conditions which we cannot as yet accurately define, produce only slight indigestion, or a diarrhœa more or less severe, or a destructive outbreak of dysentery, typhoid fever, or Asiatic cholera. I merely remark that, even in the case of the Broad Street pump water, there was, as Dr. Snow admits,† no evidence to prove the presence of choleraic matter, though the presence of organic impurities was abundantly evident. "Mr. Eley . . . had long noticed that the water became offensive both to smell and taste, after it had been kept about two days. . . . Another person had noticed for months that a film formed on the surface of the water, when it had been kept a few hours."

As, however, I have been led, in illustrating the results of individual effort, to consider the morbific influence of water contaminated by sewage, I cannot dismiss the subject without citing some striking facts which I have gleaned from public documents, or from my own experience. In July, 1849,‡ "the privies of a number of houses in Silkmill Row, Hackney, were pulled down," and the four cesspools which were substituted for them were situated respectively at the distance of one, three, five, and twelve yards from "the only well which supplies with water twelve houses containing 85 inhabitants." The water, which a fortnight later began to be offensive, was thereafter rendered "as thick as thin soup" by the admixture of sewage. Of the 85 inhabitants 22 wisely avoided the water and escaped disease, while 46 of the remaining 63 "were attacked with severe diarrhœa, one of them approaching cholera." There was no question here of cholera discharges in the cesspools, for the "row" had been and remained free from the epidemic.

"Jacob's Island,"§ a portion of the parish of Christ Church, Bermondsey, contains between 300 and 400 houses, and is surrounded by a tidal ditch or millstream, which receives the contents of the sewers and drains of all the drained houses, besides the refuse of the neighbouring houses and the contents of their privies, and was the

---

* *Association Journal*, 1854, pp. 929, 950, 974, 1152, under the signature "Common Sense;" 1855, pp. 207, 283, signed "W. Budd."

† On "The Mode of Communication of Cholera." By John Snow, M.D., Second edition, 1855. Churchill, p. 52.

‡ "Report of General Board of Health on the Epidemic Cholera of 1848 and 1849," p. 60.

§ Mr. Grainger's "Report to the General Board of Health on the Cholera of 1848 and 1849." (Appendix B.) p. 92.

sole source of the water supply of 150 houses. Many of the inhabitants were in the habit of using it for cooking, and had even drunk it unboiled during the heat of summer. Such being the case, need we wonder that "dyspepsia, cachexia, a peculiar 'sickness of stomach,' and irritable bowels are at all times very prevalent;" that in 1832 and 1849 the earliest fatal cases of cholera occurred close to this ditch, and that in the latter year diarrhœa was universal, and cholera carried off 61 victims.

Dr. Acland's statements* regarding the water supply of Oxford are singularly interesting and conclusive. "The southern parishes," he says, "suffered in 1854 nearly twice as much as in 1832, but only a sixth more than in 1849. The water supply was bad; some of the wells were foul to a degree; one stank; some were dry; and the city water, wherever distributed, was unfit for use at such a time." 'In 1832 there were, out of 174 cases in all Oxford, in the parish of St. Clement's alone 74 cases of cholera, and in 1849 only three. During the former epidemic the inhabitants had filthy water from a sewer-receiving stream, and in 1849 from the springs of Headington, conveyed thither,' with the like results as in Exeter soon after 1832. 'In 1854, out of 194 cases, but 18 occurred in St. Clement's; a proportional increase which would tend to show, what indeed we have various other evidence of, that the water supply, though it may be one mode, is not the only mode of conveying the cholera poison.' The case of the county gaol, one of the few prisons in which cholera has prevailed, is peculiarly instructive. It is not far from the city prison, 'is admirably managed' by attentive humane officers, and has an accomplished practitioner for its surgeon, yet has been visited during each epidemic with diarrhœa and cholera, from which the city prison has always been exempt. In the county gaol there were three cases of cholera in 1832, and 14 in 1849; and in 1854, during the fortnight which preceded the inquiry into the state of the water supply on the 29th of September, 'there had occurred 20 cases of choleraic diarrhœa, and five cases of cholera, of which four were fatal.' That branch of the river which flows near the gaol, passes through the Castle Mill, above which it is dammed up for the mill-head. The water, when the mill is at work, forms a brisk stream in the mill-tail, which becomes a nearly stagnant pool when the mill is not working. Into this pool, already much contaminated, the sewage of the prison was conveyed by a drain, within 10 feet of the mouth of which 'the supply pipe sucked up the contents of the pool for the prison use.' With the water thus obtained, 'the soup and the gruel, important articles in the weekly diet, were made.' The pipes were immediately cut off, and only three cases of choleraic diarrhœa and one of cholera (none being fatal) were reported during the rest of the epidemic."

This Oxford episode occurred during a season of epidemic visitation, and remarkable for drought and intense heat: here is another

---

* Memoir on the Cholera at Oxford in the year 1854. pp. 39, 51, 52.

which occurred in the depth of winter. Few Londoners can have forgotten the great snow-storm of January, 1866. A partial thaw was succeeded by a very sharp frost, and that again on the 11th of January by a gale of wind, another heavy snow-fall, and an exceedingly rapid thaw. The outlet of the large Knightsbridge sewer, being then very small, was soon choked up, and the contents overflowed through the traps into the areas and kitchens of many of the neighbouring houses. Several families drew their supply of drinking water from a favourite private pump hard by. On the 14th it was slate-coloured and smelt offensive; but as on the 17th it looked and smelt perfectly pure, most of the members of the various households again partook of it freely. That night all who had used it were seized with more or less violent diarrhœa, in one case profuse, with obstinate vomiting, closely resembling cholera, and followed next day by extreme and helpless prostration. Those who did not make use of it escaped. The water, when tested with nitrate of silver, was found, notwithstanding its seeming purity, to be "highly charged with organic matter—in fact, with sewage." The well was pumped dry, after which the water was twice tested, and found free from organic impurities.

My next and concluding instance illustrates very strikingly one mode in which typhoid fever may be propagated, and perhaps originated. I agree with my distinguished friend and late colleague, Dr. Murchison, that this very fatal form of fever commonly arises from the emanations of cesspools and sewers, and am disposed to admit that the discharges from typhoid patients, which Dr. Budd regards as highly infectious, and indeed the only medium of infection, may in certain circumstances propagate the disease. Here, however, was neither cesspool nor sewer gas; nor does it appear likely that in the first instance there was any typhoid patient to produce the specific poison*—but simply the admixture of ordinary sewage with the drinking water, which, partaken of by the inmates of a large establishment, produced a frightful outbreak of typhoid or enteric fever. At Bishopstoke in Hampshire, where a small number of the intelligent residents have for some time been struggling resolutely, but as yet vainly, in favour of a system of sewerage, which the vestry and the Winchester board of guardians consider a needless luxury in a place containing 500 or 600 inhabitants, there was in May, 1866, a ladies' boarding school, which contained 28 inmates, and had up to that time had a perfectly clean bill of health. During the previous nine years, at all events, there had not been such a thing as a case of fever in the establishment, which has no cesspool in or near it, the sewage having long been conveyed by a pipe drain into the Itchen. The water was obtained from a spring on the premises, was

---

* The mother of one of the servants was ill in the village, before the outbreak, of a low fever, said *not* to have been typhoid; but she states positively that neither before her illness, nor during her convalescence, was she within the school. There was no other case of fever in the neighbourhood.

always filtered before being used, and had been analysed not long before, and found quite pure. The circumstances connected with this analysis are singular and very interesting. I state them in the words of my friend, Dr. Parkes, of Netley, who "saw three of the young ladies frequently," and certifies them all to have been "cases of very severe and unequivocal typhoid fever." "An officer at Netley," writes Dr. Parkes, "being about to place two daughters at this school, made a careful inspection of the building. At the end of it, he said to the schoolmistress, 'I like everything connected with your school, but one thing. I have found out that your drain pipe runs close to your well.' (It was only three feet distant.) 'The lady replied that as the well water was perfectly good, she did not think it could be so, or at least that no harm had ever resulted. Major —— replied, 'I have heard so much at Netley of the dangers of such an arrangement that I don't like it.' Before placing his daughters there, he obtained some of the water, and I had it analysed for him; it was quite pure. Subsequently he obtained some more, and this was also analysed and found to be quite pure. Major —— sent his daughters to the school; both had the fever which afterwards broke out, and one of them died." One of the young ladies fell ill and continued so for a week, when she seemed to get better, but felt weak and was easily fagged. She was again attacked on the 20th of June, and had a very severe illness. A second fell ill on the 27th of May, and died on the 27th of June. Between the date of her seizure and the beginning of July, not fewer than 18 out of the 28 inmates were successively attacked. The last case, after an illness of about six weeks, also died on the 18th of August. In two other cases, (*i.e.*, in four out of eighteen) the disease likewise proved fatal. What could be the origin of so severe, and so thoroughly localised, an outbreak of enteric fever? About the 7th of June the water was noticed to have a nasty taste, and from that day its use was discontinued. A careful examination showed that, owing to heavy rains, there had been a subsidence of the soil beneath the drain pipe, which had given way, so as to permit the sewage to escape and gradually to soak through the intervening three feet of earth, till a free run was established between the drain and the well, the water being now found, on re-examination, to contain a large amount of organic impurity." An instructive commentary on the proposal which was at one time made, that those who live at the top of the rising ground on which the village is built, and at some distance from the river, should sink pits for their sewage through the clay, and let it "lose itself," as the phrase is, in the gravel! But what if, instead of losing itself, it should find its way into the springs, and so poison the whole water supply of the neighbourhood? There are many things in heaven and earth not dreamt of in the philosophy of vestrymen and parish surveyors; and one of these is that "out of sight," though "out of mind," does not always mean out of existence.

To return from this long, but far from needless digression, Dr. Snow is by no means a solitary instance of self-devotion to the cause of sanitary improvement. So far back as 1833, Mr. Robert Baker, the factory inspector, then a public-spirited citizen and councillor of Leeds, led the way in exhibiting the monstrous evils, for which, more recently, Dr. Greenhow and Dr. Julian Hunter* in their official reports, and Mr. James Hole, in his deeply interesting work on "The Homes of the Working Classes,"† have held up Leeds and its obstinately obstructive authorities to the wonder and reprobation of the United Kingdom. I regret that I have not had the advantage of perusing Mr. Baker's earlier reports ‡ on the condition of the great industrial metropolis of the West Riding of Yorkshire; but it is highly instructive—as showing for how long a period in this nineteenth century a proved and criminal neglect may be resolutely persevered in, notwithstanding the wholesale destruction of life and morals occasioned thereby—to compare his very able and exhaustive report in 1842§ with the statements of Dr. Greenhow in 1858, of Dr. Julian Hunter, in 1865, and of Mr. Hole in 1866. I make no apology for giving in parallel columns the following savoury extracts, which I request my readers carefully to peruse, that they may understand the enormity of the evils which are often shielded from view by the convenient plea of "the right of self-government." I am happy to think that the picture is now, or will soon be, one of the past, as the recent appointment of so resolute and able an officer of health as Dr. Robinson, affords a guarantee that the local authorities are now at length in earnest about the purification of Leeds.

<table>
<tr><td>BAKER in 1842.</td><td>GREENHOW in 1858.</td></tr>
</table>

BAKER in 1842.

"Along the line of these two wards, and down the street which divides them, and where this sewer has recently been made, numbers of streets have been formed, and houses erected, without pavement, and hence without surface drainage, without sewers, or, if under-drainage can be called sewers, then with such as, becoming choked in a few months, are even worse than if they were altogether without. The surface of these streets is considerably elevated by accumulated ashes and filth, untouched by any scavenger; they form nuclei of disease exhaled from a thousand sources. Here and there stagnant water and channels so offensive that they have been declared to be unbearable, lie under the doorways of the uncomplaining poor; and

GREENHOW in 1858.

"Leeds is of course traversed by certain principal streets; but these are fewer than is common in other great towns, and the interspaces between these principal roads are occupied by dense complicated congeries of narrow and often ill-kept streets and courts, which have but seldom been adopted as highways by the municipal authorities, are often in a very foul state, and, according to Mr. Sanderson, the local inspector, are neither kept in order nor cleansed at the public expense. Many of these by-streets are neither paved nor drained, and very often they are so imperfectly channelled, that surface water remains stagnant on them until dried up by the influence of the sun and wind. Sometimes these streets have no outlet at the further end, being

---

* "Second and Eighth Reports of the Medical Officer of the Privy Council," 1859 and 1855.

† "A Chapter on Leeds." pp. 123-144.

‡ In 1833, 1838, 1839, and 1840, referred to by Mr. Hole, p. 123 *et seq.*

§ "Local Reports on the Sanitary Condition of the Labouring Population of England and Wales, 1842," pp. 348-409.

privies so laden with ashes and excrementitious matter as to be unuseable, prevail, till the streets themselves become offensive from deposits of this description; in short, there is generally pervading these localities a want of the common decencies of life." (*Local Reports*, 1842, p 352.)

Of one noted *cul-de-sac* he says, " the name of this place is the Boot and Shoe Yard, in Kirkgate, a location, from whence the Commissioners removed, in the days of the cholera, 75 cart loads of manure which had been untouched for years, and where there now exists a surface of human excrement of very considerable extent, to which these impure and unventilated dwellings are additionally exposed." p 353.

" The contractor for the street sweepings, who is the treater with the Commissioners of Public nuisances in Leeds, absolutely rented and rents, or did rent a very few weeks ago, a plot of vacant land in the centre of North East Ward, the largest ward, in point of population, of the whole township of Leeds, and containing the greatest number of poor, as a depôt for the sweepings from the streets and markets, both vegetable and general, for the purpose of exsiccating and accumulating till they could be sold as manure and carried away. So noisome were these exhalations, that the inhabitants complained of their utter inability to ventilate their sleeping-rooms during the day time, and of the insufferable stench to which both by day and night they were subjected. "A great many of the privies of the cottages are built in small passages, between clumps of houses which are different properties; others, with the ash entrance open to the public streets; and others at a little distance from and open to the front of the houses; whilst some streets are entirely without. The inhabitants, to use the language of an old woman of whom inquiry was made, says that 'they do as they can, and make use of the streets as the common receptacle.' These remarks apply in particular to three streets of Leeds, which contain a population of between 400 and 500 persons, where there is not a useable privy for the whole number." p. 356.

in fact mere *culs de sac;* more frequently they communicate one with another, so as to form a complicated labyrinth of very imperfectly ventilated little streets and courts. Houses in such situations are very commonly indeed built back to back, and even when not so they are often destitute of windows in the rear, and possess no efficient means of thorough ventilation. The streets of Leeds have in fact been laid out and the houses erected according to the caprice or interest of their owners, without reference to the health, comfort and convenience of the inhabitants, or to the fact that they were destined to form integral parts of a great town. The courts of Leeds are rarely spacious and airy, are sometimes entered through covered passages, and are by no means always clean, but more frequently are unpaved and in bad condition. Privies are almost universal, and are, from their position in relation to dwellings, the most prominent sanitary defect of the town, water closets being unknown among the poorer classes. As is common in other manufacturing towns, a single privy usually serves for several families. The situation of the privies is often most objectionable; in many of the smaller streets they are placed beneath inhabited rooms; in others they are sometimes placed against the walls of houses, or so near to them that the effluvia are felt within doors, and infect many of the courts and smaller streets. Although certainly not the exclusive cause of diarrhœa, yet upon the whole that disease has been the most rife and most fatal in streets where the privy nuisance prevails in an aggravated form."—" Second Report of Medical Officer of Privy Council," 1859, p. 134.

HUNTER in 1865 and 1866.

"To the eye of an inspector who had just left Newcastle and Sunderland, and who in the same week visited Sheffield, Leeds, in August, 1865, presented a surprising sight, bringing to remembrance the condition of many English towns of twenty years ago, but finding hardly any standard with which to be compared in the present state of any great town. Thousands of tons of midden filth filled the receptacles, scores of tons lay strewn about where the receptacles would receive no more. Hundreds of people, long unable to use the privy because of the rising heap, were depositing on the floors. A few dawdling carts, under command of Mr. Sands, the corporation officer, and subject to no inspection, unless Mr. Sands be taken to be inspector of his own duties, would, after many applications, relieve the middens of such inhabitants as could, by peremptory manner or by influence obtain a hearing. Even then the relief was most imperfect. In one instance the scavenger reported a receptacle as emptied, yet twenty tons of stuff were removed when a second visit was insisted on. The pressure of these enormous weights was so great that liquid ordure had been seen, after penetrating the ground, to be forced up around the hearthstones of neighbouring cottages. The officers of the union complained to their board no less than 3,500 times, in about two years and a half, of distinct instances of neglect.

"The force employed in cleaning, which had been last spring forty-five carts, had been reduced to thirty, and with an excess of delicacy, badly agreeing with the universal neglect, no removals were made except by night. Such carts as were employed only carried the midden filth to a deposit in the town, by the water side, except a few by which some railway trucks were loaded. At this deposit stood thousands of tons of midden filth needlessly waiting for removal by boat or cart for consumption; 7,000 tons stood there at one time this year, and yet the quantity at this moment found to be necessary is and need never exceed one hundred tons. Boxes which receive closet manure from manufactories are here emptied in large numbers, and though both at the original receptacles and at the deposit itself a

HOLE in 1866.

"To crown the imperfect construction of these dwellings, they are placed in immediate contact with privies and cesspools, which, although seldom noticed by the inhabitants, are utterly intolerable to a stranger. Then, again, the supply of privies is quite inadequate for the ordinary requirements of decency, and many of them are under bedrooms. p. 127.

"'On Sunday mornings,' says a woman, 'the neighbours have to watch and wait for a chance of getting into the conveniences!' In one of the above streets the privies have pigsties beside them! How intolerable the stench, particularly in hot weather, the reader may conceive. p. 128.

"Owing to a recent increase of fever and of the death-rate, meetings to consider the sanitary state of Leeds have been held in every ward, at which clergymen and others cognizant of the facts agreed in showing that there was serious neglect; that numerous ashpits were filled to overflowing in immediate proximity with the houses of the poor, and that gully-holes in the streets had been closed up for months.

"'We saw,' says one of the visitors in Hunslet, 'places that had been full for weeks, not of ashes, but of fluid matter, up to the seat, so that the women in the houses said they had to empty everything into the streets. In one yard, consisting of twenty-six houses belonging to one landlord, there are two privies only, and an open drain down the centre. A school of sixty boys adjoins the privies, and the ashpit is only about four feet high. In another yard, belonging to the same landlord, there are thirty-two houses to two privies, and the yard itself is saturated with disgusting matter." p. 129.

"We can point to numerous pigsties which have existed more than thirty years, in close proximity to dwellings in the very centre of the town, and which still flourish as redolent as ever." p. 130.

deodorizing powder was freely used, the place emitted a strong fæcal stench, doing its best to warn the corporation of the mischief they were doing." (Eighth Report of the Medical Officer of the Privy Council, p. 234.)

"The orifice of the midden was even in large highways often turned to the street, and often unprotected by any door. There were properties without any privies or ashpits at all, yet quite within the town.

"On the 26th of May, 1866, the justices ordered the removal of the Waterloo depôt; the town clerk appeared to beg delay." p. 236.

Happily, as we shall see, the "ancient reign" of the pigs and piggeries in Leeds has now been effectually disturbed, and we have been lately reminded, by a letter in the *Times** from Dr. Fowler in reference to the state of privies in the City of London, that Leeds is not the only place where urgent and oft-repeated complaints and remonstrances are unheeded by the local authorities.

What has been done for Leeds by those gentlemen to whose labours I have referred, has been done for Oxford by Dr. Acland, whose memoir on the Cholera in 1854† is indeed an exhaustive treatise on the then unwholesome condition of that renowned seat of learning. I shall have occasion again to refer to the interesting information with which he has lately favoured me as to its present state and prospects. Dr. Shapter's volume‡ and supplement have thrown much light on the history of the cholera at Exeter, and of the sanitary measures adopted with such encouraging success in consequence of its frightful ravages in 1832. Dr. J. C. Hall has from time to time contributed much valuable information on the state of Sheffield and the diseases prevalent there. Mr. Rendle § and Dr. Horace Jeaffreson‖ have given us precise and highly important facts regarding the principal fever haunts of London, and the mode in which they are dealt with by vestries. Dr. Tyacke has been unwearied in his efforts to stimulate the local authorities of Chichester, and Dr. Edward Wilson, failing any vigorous and comprehensive measures on the part of the Town Commissioners, has supplied us with numerous and authentic details regarding Cheltenham in his elaborate and very able paper read before the British Association for

---

* September 17th, 1866.

† "Memoir on the Cholera at Oxford in the year 1854, with Considerations suggested by the Epidemic." By Henry Wentworth Acland, M.D., F.R.S., F.R.G.S., &c. Churchill, 1856.

‡ "History of the Cholera in Exeter in 1832." Churchill, 1849.

§ "London Vestries and their Sanitary Work." By W. Rendle. Churchill, 1865. "Fever in London: its Social and Sanitary Lessons," 1866.

‖ Letters in *Times*, April 14, September 7, 1865, January 3, 27, March 5, 1866. See also leaders, April 15 and September 7, 1865, January 3, 5, 1866

the Advancement of Science in 1864.* Of the abundant labours of my friend Mr. Rumsey, also of Cheltenham, and one of our highest authorities on all matters connected with "State Medicine," it would be superfluous in me to say a word in commendation. Gloucester and Newcastle-upon-Tyne are likewise fortunate in having each an accomplished and able medical reporter. Dr. Washbourn, in the former city, has drawn up and published at his own cost five annual reports "On the Sanitary Condition of Gloucester and its Vicinity;" and Dr. Philipson, to whom I am indebted for much help heartily given, has for several years published the result of the returns sent to him by the members of the Northumberland and Durham Medical Society, in a report, which appears every two months, of the prevalent diseases of Newcastle and the whole surrounding district. As regards Manchester, the only ground of hope for future sanitary reform would seem to be the existence of its justly celebrated sanitary association,† which has for a long series of years been collecting, and classifying, and publishing in weekly, quarterly, and annual reports, which are models of their kind, a mass of details of the highest value in relation to the health of Manchester and Salford. And not only so, but they have long been endeavouring (my distinguished friend, Mr. Thomas Turner, the president, frequently taking part,) to inculcate sound sanitary and social doctrines among the working population, by courses of lectures admirably fitted to promote the end in view. They have also, from time to time, applied themselves to the more herculean task of stirring up the local authorities to the discharge of some of the more obvious responsibilities devolving upon them, as the guardians of the health of the great and prosperous community, which, by a pleasant fiction, they are presumed to govern for its good. The very striking and valuable paper entitled, "Remarks on Some of the Numerical Tests of the Health of Towns," by Messrs. Arthur Ransome and William Royston, was published by that Association in 1864; and to its honorary secretary, Dr. John Edward Morgan, we owe the very interesting and instructive paper read at Sheffield last year,‡ on "The Danger of Deterioration of Race from the too Rapid Increase of Great Cities." Though some may be inclined to fear that the *vis inertiæ* which has so long and so pertinaciously withstood such well-directed efforts, must be invincible, we cannot resist the conviction that, in the unabated vigour with which this admirable association maintains its protest against official neglect and incompetency, we have the pledge of an ultimate and complete victory.

If the zeal and energy of a few private individuals singly and in combination, and of associations, have thus been applied, with so considerable an aggregate result, to the increase of our knowledge,

---

* Since published as a pamphlet—" Sanitary Statistics of Cheltenham." Longmans, 1865.

† The Manchester and Salford Sanitary Association.

‡ *Soc. Sc. Transactions*, 1865, pp. 427 to 449. Since published by Longmans in a separate form.

and the establishment on a solid basis of the principles that should guide us in our endeavours to improve the public health, much larger contributions to our knowledge and progress have been made, first by Mr. Chadwick and his reporters throughout the country in 1842 and 1843, and during the last nine years by the medical officer of the Privy Council and his staff of very able assistants. Here we have another force *ab extra* brought to bear on the sluggishness of local bodies. After the first visitation of the cholera, the mop and pail, which had for a time been much in requisition, were by common consent laid aside, and the whole nation fell asleep in the midst of yearly-accumulating abominations, until, in the general and local reports on the sanitary condition of the labouring population of Great Britain, Mr. Chadwick and his fellow-workers held up the mirror to a multitude of foul spots both in town and country, and produced an impression of incredulous horror, which the lapse of a quarter of a century has not entirely obliterated. But it was not till 1858 that the foundation of our present system of annual reports was laid, in a small but very remarkable Blue Book,* which consists mainly of a report by Dr. Headlam Greenhow, "On the Different Prevalence of Certain Diseases in Different Districts of England and Wales," with an introductory report by Mr. Simon. The very valuable reports made in subsequent years, according to the terms of sections 5 and 6 of the "Act (1858) for vesting in the Privy Council certain powers for the protection of the public health,"† on diarrhœa, diphtheria, lung diseases, typhus, typhoid fever, and small-pox, by Dr. Greenhow, Dr. Burdon Sanderson, Dr. Buchanan, Dr. Seaton, Dr. Julian Hunter, Mr. Radcliffe, and others, have amply confirmed the soundness of the principles set forth in the preliminary papers, and have from time to time placed in the pillory, for the edification of the public, some of the more incorrigible offenders. That good has been effected by this wholesome practice of publicly recording the chief sanitary events of each year, of investigating on the spot the circumstances which have preceded and accompanied local outbreaks of epidemic and infectious disease, and of laying the result before Parliament, it would be absurd to deny. And that this work has been well and very ably done by Mr. Simon and his assistants, will, I apprehend, be universally admitted. Yet the benefit accruing therefrom has consisted much more in the collection and diffusion of authentic information, than in the communication of any decided impulse towards sanitary improvement among the great masses of the population, where preventible disease slays its annual myriads. I wish to speak guardedly on this subject, notwithstanding the special inquiries I have instituted, because I observe that Mr. Simon,‡

---

* "Papers relating to the Sanitary State of the People of England." Presented to both Houses of Parliament, by command of Her Majesty, 1858.

† 21 & 22 Vict., cap., 97.

‡ Eighth Report of the Medical Officer of the Privy Council, for 1865, pp. 18, 19.

speaking of Dr. Buchanan's investigations into the state of "places in which, for some considerable number of years, proper works of drainage and water supply have been established, or particular sanitary regulations been in force," expresses the hope that he may be able, in his next report, "to state conclusions which may be permanently valid as to the practical fruit of our best tested sanitary improvements."

Still it is impossible, while reading those very interesting and instructive records of local sluggishness and preventible mortality, to banish from one's mind the express terms of the "Diseases' Prevention Act, 1855," under which, as confirmed by "the Public Health Act, 1858," the Privy Council exercises its present functions in health matters. "Whenever (sect. 5) any part of England appears to be threatened with, or is affected by any formidable epidemic, endemic, or contagious disease, the Lords and others of her Majesty's most Honourable Privy Council, or any three or more of them, may, by order or orders to be by them from time to time made, direct that the provisions herein contained for the prevention of diseases be put in force," &c. And section 6 goes on to provide that they "may issue directions and regulations for the speedy interment of the dead; for house to house visitation; for guarding against the spread of disease, and affording to persons afflicted by or threatened with such epidemic, endemic, or contagious diseases such medical aid and such accommodation as may be required." These ample powers were plainly conferred, if words have any meaning, with the view of enabling the executive not only to prevent the introduction of epidemics from without, but to root out, if possible, those formidable and destructive diseases which have so long dwelt or are begotten in the homes of our people. They have, however, been directed so exclusively against those rare visitants, the alarm of whose approach is in itself a warning to make ready, that they are generally supposed to have no force against our bosom-vipers, which have a vested right to sting to death as many as they list, or as the "liberty of the subject" thinks proper. If cholera threatens us, if yellow fever comes to one of our seaports, if a single case of cattle plague or sheep-pox appears among our herds or flocks, forthwith "my lords" wake up into a state of preternatural activity, hourly telegrams flash to and fro, and voluminous orders fill the pages of the *Gazette*. But with the departure of these intruders the wonted quietude returns, as if there were no "formidable epidemic, endemic, or contagious disease" within our borders worthy to engage "my lords'" attention! Yet true it is that strong men and healthy women—"the breadwinners" of the nation, as Dr. Trench truly remarks—are "dying like rotten sheep" by thousands, after a fortnight's illness, of typhus, of typhoid, and of small-pox; and we think we have done our duty when we have held an inquest on the hecatombs of dead! For several years typhus has been raging epidemically in London; and in Greenock, in the west of Scotland, so virulent has been its type, and so great the mortality occasioned by it, that a special inquiry, conducted by so able an observer as **my** friend Dr. Buchanan, was reckoned necessary by the Health Department of the Privy Council.* As regards London, the statements of Dr. Horace Jeaffreson and Mr. Rendle, which recal, as they exactly tally with, my experience in the Glasgow fever hospital thirty years ago, show that its principal haunts are well known, and leave no doubt that by the timely removal of the sick, and .by emptying and thoroughly cleansing and limewashing the tenements where it has fixed its abode, this demon of our great towns might be effectually exorcised. Recent experience in Bristol, as I shall show, goes to establish the same position. Let it then be clearly understood that the means of greatly diminishing, if not of putting a stop to the ravages of typhus are within our reach ; that the Privy Council has full power to put these means in force for the public good and the preservation of life from wholesale destruction; but that, nevertheless, the Privy Council declines the responsibility of saving the lives of the lieges, against the will of interested landlords, and the prejudices of the local authorities ! Placed in this light, the phantom of " vested rights " assumes a very hideous aspect; and the *inertia* of the Privy Council seems to ordinary minds both inexplicable and inexcusable. Their function, it would appear, is calmly to watch the progress of the slaughter which they might prevent, and then " to point the moral" which dead tongues cannot enforce, and to " adorn the tale " which the victims of official prudery cannot tell. The Home Secretary, again, who is empowered by the Sanitary Act, 1866, to interfere, if he sees fit, on complaint made to him of the default of any local authority, will doubtless, as a general rule, see fit *not* to interfere, and will leave matters to right themselves.

Having thus glanced at what has, and what has not, been effected by individual and combined local effort, and by public departments under the Crown, let us next inquire what has been done by the local authorities themselves, to whom, as we have seen, belongs the duty—which they must not be enjoined to fulfil—of caring for the health of their constituents. To such an extent has the policy of non-interference been carried, that outside of London the appointment of medical officers of health is entirely optional ; and since 1860 the authorities of places under the Nuisances Removal Act are left free to appoint or not, as they may think fit, even inspectors of nuisances. Before that date their appointment was obligatory.

The fruits of this suggestive and marvellously inconsistent policy are precisely what might have been expected. In the absence of any official returns on this important subject, I first consulted what professes to be a quasi-official work, published by Knight and Co., viz., " The Union, Parish, and Health Officers' Guide for 1865." There I found that of 570 places under the Local Government Act, 1858, and the Public Health Act, 1848, with populations varying from 214 to 200,000, fifty seem to have no inspectors of nuisances;

---

* Eighth Report, &c. pp. 209-220.

153 have each one; 16 have two; and four have three inspectors of nuisances; while in 347, one man holds the double office either of surveyor and inspector of nuisances, or of inspector and collector, or unites in himself all the three offices of surveyor, inspector, and collector. It struck me as strange that small places with not more than 800 inhabitants should have two inspectors, while large towns, such as Brighton, Bradford, Merthyr Tydfil, Nottingham, Portsmouth, and Sunderland, with populations varying from 50,000 to 106,218, have no more than two; and yet more strange that Preston, with 86,000, Bristol with 154,000, and Sheffield with 200,000 of a population, should have only one! And what is *one* among so many? I found also that in 92—one-sixth of the 570 places enumerated—officers of health had been appointed, and it struck me as very strange that 63 of these held office in places whose population was under 10,000, while only 29 remained for towns with large populations; and 111 towns with populations varying from 20,000 to 200,000 had no officer of health at all. These results, obtained with much labour and expenditure of time, seemed to me too startling to be trustworthy; and the Privy Council reports contained scarcely a syllable in reference to this subject, on which one would think they ought to contain the fullest and most accurate information. I accordingly sought a check in the "Municipal Corporations' Directory," a work very recently published, and containing much useful information; but I found, after a very careful examination, that while every other officer, however insignificant, is thought worthy of insertion, medical officers of health scarcely ever appear, not even those in the metropolis being inserted; and inspectors of nuisances are very often awanting. I enter into these details for a special reason, viz., to demonstrate the necessity of having an annual Parliamentary return of all these officers, of the population and extent of the districts under their supervision, of the duties devolving upon them, and of the salaries paid to them. Such a return would shew us at a glance which places we should take an example from, and which, again, should be made examples of, and would form an indispensable preliminary to sound and comprehensive legislation.

Baffled in the quarters to which I have referred, but considering it essential to have thoroughly accurate and trustworthy information on a subject of so great importance, I felt that I must myself undertake this parliamentary inquiry, and commenced correspondence, as my distinguished friend Mr. Rumsey did before publishing his work on "State Medicine," with some of the many friends whom I have the privilege of knowing in London and throughout the country. I also ventured to apply to not a few to whom I must have been entirely unknown, in the hope that the freemasonry which exists among those who have a common object and end in view would not only excuse my boldness, but respond to my appeal. The result proves that I was not mistaken, for in only one case out of more than a hundred have I been disappointed of a return; and these have generally been prompt, always clear and cordial, and often full. The best thank-offering I can present to those who have so kindly trusted me is to gather up and exhibit some of the fruits of this inquiry.

And first, as regards the metropolitan district, which, as having been for eleven years under the compulsory provisions of the Metropolis Local Management Act, many reckon a pattern to be held up for the imitation of the whole country. How far this impression is warranted by facts, let the tabular statement in Table I., compiled from the most authentic sources, bear witness.

Let me endeavour, as briefly as possible, to extract the full meaning of this table. And first about the double column for population. After carefully constructing my table and striking my averages from the local returns, I found, on comparing them with the Registrar General's Summary for 1866, that the discrepancies in particular districts were so great as to necessitate the entire reconstruction of my table. Though the general result is not much affected thereby, I have exhibited the two returns side by side, as showing most conclusively how important it is that the health officers and the Registrar-General should compare notes together, so as to ensure accuracy in the local death-rates.

The metropolitan district, with a population of above three millions, has 47 medical officers of health, or, on an average, one to 64,500; or, deducting the population of Woolwich, which has no health officer, one to every 63,630 inhabitants. According to the Registrar-General's statement of the population, there is one to 64,638; or, excluding Woolwich, one to 63,630. This general average, however, gives no idea of the immense disparity existing between the districts both in extent and populousness; for while, at the one end of the scale, there are three with scattered populations of 4,000, 7,500, and 10,000 respectively, there are three at the other end with dense populations of 163,000, 191,000, and 211,000. The number of inspectors of nuisances for this enormous and rapidly growing population is nominally 100; in the proportion, after deducting Mile End and Woolwich, from which I have no returns, of one to 29,000 inhabitants. Nominally, I say, for it must not be forgotten that the whole time of one, and most of the time of eleven others, is occupied in doing work unconnected with sanitary matters. If, then, we reckon these twelve as equivalent to five efficient inspectors of nuisances (a very liberal allowance), we have not more than 93 inspectors for the three millions of inhabitants, and the 78,800 acres of area, of the metropolitan district; or one to 31,300 inhabitants. But here, again, the disparity of the districts is immense; for while two sub-districts, with populations of 4,000 and 10,000 respectively, have each the services of one inspector under the control of the medical officer, St. Marylebone and St. Pancras, with their widely extended areas, and with populations respectively of 163,000 and 211,000, have each of them only two; and the services of two half-inspectors are available for Greenwich with 97,000, and Shoreditch with 136,000 inhabitants! In some districts, viz., Shoreditch (which has declined to take up the Sanitary Act, 1866), Streatham and Putney, the sub-inspectors engaged during the prevalence of cholera, under the orders of the Privy Council, have been discharged. In Hampstead, Wandsworth, Clapham, and Battersea, one of the two then engaged for each sub-district has been retained for a time; while, in Camberwell and in Chelsea, the local boards have had the good sense to retain the whole staff of inspectors, a measure which is producing the most satisfactory results. In Chelsea, Dr. Barclay informs me, the inhabitants have already discovered that the removal of nuisances by the vestry officials is a reality, instead of a sham, as has too commonly been the case when ordinary dustmen have been charged with its execution.

As regards the performance of the work assigned to them, one great outstanding fact stamps the character and spirit of the Metropolitan Medical Officers of Health. Their union—for most of them belong to it—in a society which meets weekly for discussion and interchange of information on all subjects of general and present interest to the health of the community, has made them a power in the State, of so considerable influence, that recalcitrant vestrymen, scandalized at the spectacle of the servants presuming to take counsel together, and to dictate to their masters, have repeatedly threatened them with censure or dismissal. It is very plain that these gentlemen, who, in addition to the fatigues of their daily practice, thus voluntarily undertake so serious an additional burden, in the interest not of themselves but of the public, are thoroughly in earnest in the work they have in hand; and the presumption is strongly in favour of an efficient discharge of the duties of the office, so far as that depends on their personal efforts, and is consistent with the exigencies of private practice. But the officer of health, even if unencumbered with the cares and distractions of an extensive and laborious practice, is neither an Argus nor a Briareus, with a hundred eyes to spy out and a hundred hands to remove the nuisances of his district. The inspector of nuisances is, or ought to be, the right hand of the officer of health, to whose usefulness, if he be backed by the local authority and aided by a thoroughly efficient staff of inspectors, it would be rash to set limits.

If, however, the local authorities, acting as if the officer of health were to be his own inspector, decline to appoint more than one sanitary inspector for districts containing 30,000, 60,000, 80,000, 100,000, 120,000, or even 136,000 inhabitants; if, moreover, they render that one inspector independent of the officer of health, or, acknowledging his partial responsibility to that gentleman, so burden him with other duties that anything like efficient inspection of nuisances becomes an impossibility—what is the conclusion we are forced to draw? Plainly, that, whoever may be in earnest about the removal of nuisances and the improvement of the public health, such local authorities are not so. I cannot better exhibit the full force of the evidence afforded by this table as to the utter inadequacy of the inspection to which many of the most crowded and unhealthy districts of the metropolis are now subjected, than by quoting the following very instructive passage from Mr. Rendle's paper on " Fever in London : its Social and Sanitary Lessons."

" In the next parish to mine are 8,603 farmed houses, and but one inspector. In May, 1865, according to a return I have, the City of London, St. Pancras, Marylebone, Lambeth, Islington, had each but two inspectors ; St. Leonard's, Shoreditch, only one. Of course it is impossible to do the work, and get rid of the fever-producing causes in this way. I have vestry lists of cases for sanitary improvement. With one inspector, who gave part of his time to sanitary work, average of two lists of places requiring work to be done, 31. After the appointment of one additional inspector, average of two lists, 315 cases. Lambeth is now seriously debating on the appointment of two additional inspectors ; so is St. Pancras."

It appears, from the returns furnished to me, that the " serious debates " spoken of by Mr. Rendle have issued in the appointment of one more inspector for Lambeth, which has now three to its 176,000 inhabitants, while St. Pancras, with its 211,000, and St. Marylebone, with 163,000, have still only two a-piece. In Islington, however, on the earnest representation of my friend and former colleague, Dr. Edward Ballard, the able and energetic officer of health for that district, two have lately been added. In London proper, including " East London, West London, and London City," of the Registrar-General's Summary, there are eight, of whom five look after the town districts, and one takes charge of the shipping, while two are set apart for the inspection of meat, slaughter-houses, and common lodgings, the whole staff being entirely under the direction and control of so accomplished a chief as Dr. Letheby. Whitechapel is also provided with four inspectors, under the able superintendence of my friend Mr. Liddle. Bethnal Green, Bow, Hackney, Limehouse, Poplar, St. Giles and St. George's, Bloomsbury, and St. James's Westminster, have each three, though in Limehouse they are burdened with many other duties, and in several other districts their time is chiefly occupied about the streets and roads. Of Camberwell, with its four, and Chelsea with its seven inspectors, I have already spoken. The latter is, in this respect, the model district of the metropolis, for while some of the outlying sub-districts, with extensive areas and rapidly growing populations, have one inspector to from 4,000 to 9,000 inhabitants, it alone has one inspector to every 9,000 of its population. With such a staff it is not wonderful, as Dr. Barclay expresses it, that nuisances are not only inspected but removed ; while Mr. Rendle's experience shows that with one—or a part of one—inspector to a population of 55,000, the apparent freedom from nuisances arises from their not being looked for. The excellent practical result of this policy in whitening the outside of the sepulchre, while the " dead men's bones and all uncleanness " are festering within, is well understood and acted on throughout the country. It is, I am informed on unquestionable authority, a common practice for local authorities throughout England to appoint a relieving officer inspector of nuisances for an extensive district—his duties as a poor-law official being more than sufficient to occupy his whole time—and to give him a few pounds at Christmas, in consideration of his important services in hiding from the public gaze those evils against which he is supposed to wage a war of extermination. I have already hinted that one of the most ingenious devices for neutralizing the influence of the officer of health is to make the sanitary inspector wholly, or in great part, independent of his control. I invite special attention to the fact that in not fewer than fifteen districts or sub-districts of the metropolitan area, this most faulty arrangement prevails. When such are the relations between them, it depends entirely on the inspector whether he shall co-operate heartily with the health officer, or treat his wishes and suggestions with systematic neglect. It is difficult to imagine a system more likely to produce a dead lock in the working of the sanitary machinery than this.

I very much regret that, owing to the absence of a full return from that district, I am unable to complete this valuable and suggestive table by filling in the number of inspectors employed in the extensive and densely populated parish of Mile End Old Town. Woolwich, it appears from the Registrar-General's summary, is still without an officer of health. I conclude, therefore, that the sanitary concerns of its 47,363 inhabitants are still in a double sense *overlooked* by a single officer, who is supposed to be at once surveyor and inspector of nuisances.

Before dismissing the sanitary arrangements of the metropolitan district I must offer a few remarks in reference to the salaries paid to the medical officers of health. These vary from £50 to £600. It is a fact worthy of special record, that not less than eight out of forty-seven able and highly educated gentlemen receive £50 of annual salary for discharging the duties of the highest sanitary office under the local boards of this great metropolis! The salary of one of these gentlemen, and that of another in a neighbouring district, were originally £75, but were reduced to £50. The former is still on the reduced allowance, while the latter has been lately reinstated in his original salary. Yet another, with the oversight of a population of 30,000, spread over an area of about 5,000 acres, receives seventy guineas (£73 10s.) for a year's labours. So that ten out of the forty-seven medical officers of health of the metropolitan district are at this moment in receipt of salaries at and under £75 per annum! The grand total expended annually on officers of health in this vast capital, with property assessed at an annual value of above fifteen and a quarter millions, is under £8,000. The average salary of the whole forty-seven is £168 16s. But deducting six who receive from £300 to £600, and whose united salaries amount to £2,250, the average annual remuneration of the remaining forty-one is exactly £139 16s. 7d. In Bethnal Green and St. Martin's-in-the-Fields, sums of £150 and £105 respectively have been voted to the officers of health for their valuable services during the late epidemic of cholera; but a proposal recently made to vote £100 to my friend, Mr. Lord, for his labours during the late outbreak of cholera at Hampstead, was negatived.

But it is not only the salary of the officer of health that is dependent on the goodwill, or the whim, of the local board. He holds his office during their good pleasure, and the very efficiency with which he performs his duties may be an unpardonable sin in the eyes of a majority of his masters. His statements of fact may touch the interests of some, his suggestions of remedies may excite the displeasure of others, his unwelcome enunciations of great principles may create a general commotion; and if the soundness of his position cannot be assailed by reasoning, passion may suggest—as it has before now suggested—a reduction of salary, or a threat of dismissal, as likely to bring the offender to his senses. Even when no such unseemly exhibitions of temper are made, the simple plan is to let the report and suggestions of the health officer lie unheeded on the table. It would be curious and instructive to know how often the valuable results of long and laborious inquiries have thus been quietly shelved, to the detriment of the public, and in defiance of the intentions of the legislature. I am well aware that in some—perhaps not a few—instances, a very different spirit prevails, and the local authority gives a hearty support to its officer of health. But the undoubted fact that it is often otherwise proves the absolute necessity of a change of measures, if our sanitary progress is not to be indefinitely checked by the passive resistance of ignorance and unreasoning prejudice. What these measures are I defer pointing out, until I shall have given a summary of the evidence I have received from many large towns in England, and from a few in Scotland and in Wales.

I have received returns from 59 towns, with populations varying from 8,000 to 483,000, seven only having less than 20,000, and thirty-one having from 40,000 to 483,000 inhabitants. Indeed fourteen of the latter group have above 100,000, and two more respectively 97,800 and 96,800 inhabitants. It will be seen, from these figures, that, though many towns from which I could have wished to obtain information do not appear in my tables, those which are contained in them include a very large proportion of the principal towns of the kingdom, and give a fair representation of our actual sanitary condition. Of the entire number 51 are in England, four in Scotland, and four in Wales. The best guarantee I can give of the trustworthiness of my information is to record the names of those gentlemen who have so kindly furnished it.

Town.	Reporter.
Aberdare.	Mr. David Davies, O. H.
Aberdeen.	Dr. Ogston.
Bath.	Dr. R. W. Falconer.*
Birkenhead.	Mr. C. G. Mott, chairman of Health Committee, and Dr. M. K. Robinson, late O. H.

Town.	Reporter.
Birmingham . .	. . Dr. Alfred Hill, Borough Analyst, through Mr. Watkin Williams.
Bradford. . . .	. . Clerk of Board of Guardians, through Mr. Wm. Dunlop.
Brighton. . . . . :	. Mr. J. Cordy Burrows.*
Bristol and Clifton. . .	. Mr. David Davies, O. H., through Dr. Henry Marshall.
Cambridge.	. Dr. P. W. Latham.
Canterbury	. Dr. Alfred Lochée.
Cardiff	. Dr. H. J. Paine, O. H.
Carlisle.	. Wm. B. Page, through Dr. Goodfellow.
Cheltenham	. Mr. H. W. Rumsey and Dr. Wilson.
Chester	. Mr. John D. Weaver.
Chichester.	. Dr. Tyacke.
Derby	. . Dr. Wm. Ogle.
Devonport	. Mr. Paul W. Swain.
Doncaster	. Mr. Francis C. Fairbank, O. H.
Dundee.	. Dr. Robert Cocks.
Edinburgh	. Dr. Littlejohn, O. H., through Dr. Warburton Begbie.
Exeter	. Mr. P. C. Delagarde.
Gateshead.	. Dr. Wm. Robinson, O. H. through Dr. G. H. Philipson.
Glasgow	. Dr. Wm. T. Gairdner, O. H.
Gloucester	. Dr. Washbourn.
Greenock	. Dr.Wm. J. Marshall, through Rev. John McFarlan
Grimsby	. Mr. H. M. Leppington.*
Halifax	. Through Mr. W. Dunlop, of Bradford.
Hastings and St. Leonard's-on-Sea	Dr. Blakiston, F.R.S.
Hereford	. Mr. C. Lingen.
Hull	. Dr. Henry Munroe.
King's Lynn	. Dr. John Lowe.
Leeds	. Dr. M. K. Robinson, O. H., late of Birkenhead.
Leicester	. Dr. John Barclay, and Mr. Moore, O. H.
Lincoln.	. Clerk of Local Board, through Mr. R. S. Harvey.
Liverpool	. Dr. W. S. Trench, O. H.
Maidstone	. Dr. John W. Woodfall, J.P.
Manchester	. Sanitary Association, through Mr. Arthur Ransome.
Merther Tydfil	Mr. Thomas J. Dyke, O. H.
Newcastle-upon-Tyne .	. Dr. G. H. Philipson, and clerk of Public Health Committee.
Newport (Monmouth) .	. Dr. Benj. Davies, O. H.
Northampton	. Dr. John M. Bryan.
Norwich	. Mr. Wm. Cadge.
Nottingham	. Dr. Tindal Robertson.
Oxford.	. Dr. H. W. Acland. F.R.S.
Paisley . . . . . ,	. Dr. Richmond, O. H., through Dr. Wm McKechnie.
Plymouth.	. Dr. Cookworthy, and Mr. J. H. Eccles.
Portsmouth	. Mr. H. Burford Norman.
Reading	. Mr. T. L. Walford, O. H., through Mr. George May, Jun.
Salford	Sanitary Association, through Mr. Ransome.
Sheffield . . .	. Dr. John Charles Hall.
Shewsbury	. Dr. Styrap.
Southampton	. Dr. Wiblin.
South Shields . . .	. Mr. Leonard Armstrong, through Dr. Philipson.

Town.	*Reporter.*
Stafford.	Dr. Henry Day.
Sunderland.	Dr. Yeld, O. H., through Dr. Philipson.
Tynemouth.	Mr. Procter, chairman of Sanitary Commissioners, through Dr. Headlam Greenhow.
Wolverhampton. . . .	Mr. E. J. Hayes, Town Clerk.
Worcester.	Mr. H. W. Carden.
York.	Mr. W. D. Husband.*

Of the fifty-nine towns here enumerated eighteen only have regularly appointed and permanent officers of health. In five others appointments have lately been made under pressure, but only for periods of two or three months, and with temporary salaries attached to them. I place these towns, as giving no guarantee for the permanence of their present arrangements, in a separate group (A. Table II.) Group B again represents those local authorities who have, some of them many years ago, others very recently, "put their hands to the plough and are not looking back." A glance at the column which tells when the office was instituted is in itself very instructive. Of the twenty-three towns included in both groups, nine had officers of health before the commencement of 1864, while in eight of the remaining fourteen they were first appointed between April and August, 1866. So true is it that great epidemics are epochs of sanitary development, the threatened visitation of cholera having been the efficient cause of almost all of the recent appointments. But in some of these towns the development is marked apparently by a hesitation which bodes ill for the permanency of the recent reform, and certainly by a notable amount of caution and thriftiness—virtues which are supposed by some to have their favourite abode to the north of the Tweed, but which seem to flourish well in some parts of England. For instance, Lincoln, Maidstone, and Oxford, moved solely by the fear of a visit of the cholera, have each appointed an officer of health for three months ; Maidstone, as if to remind him that he is a tenant-at-will, at a salary of 10s. 6d. a day, Oxford at fifty guineas for three months' service, while Wolverhampton, more openhanded, rewards two months' hard labour with £50. Lincoln and Reading, on the other hand, cannily decline to commit themselves by fixing any salary at all. The meaning whereof might be interpreted in all these cases to be, that the departure of the cholera will be the signal for a retrograde movement, and a contented subsidence into their former blindfold security—and dirt. But Dr. Acland writes to me words of good and hopeful augury concerning Oxford. After mentioning various evils which call loudly for redress, *e.g.* the deficient drainage, the pollution of rivers by sewage, and the insufficient water supply, he proceeds :—

---

* These four gentlemen, eminent in their profession, have all held the office of Mayor in their respective towns, with the sanitary condition of which they are thoroughly conversant.

"But all these and many other evils, such as whole streets with cess-pools and wells adjoining, will now be abated. After many years' battling, public opinion is aroused, and the Sanitary Act has come just in time to clench its decisions. The Local Board has been this summer very active. Disinfectants have been largely applied in all directions during this summer by the medical officer Dr. Child, under the advice of Professor Rolleston. I make no doubt, but that in a few years, with the help of the Sanitary Act and with the co-operation of the university and the city, all that is to be desired will be effected. But it has been a tardy process here as elsewhere." All honour to those—foremost among them Drs. Acland and Rolleston—who have fought the long battle. Let us hope that the tardy victory is near, but act as if it were still far distant. So likewise in regard to Wolverhampton, respecting which I have received full and interesting details from Mr. E. J. Hayes, the able and judicious town clerk, to whom, if only he were armed with despotic powers, one would gladly see entrusted the sanitary organization of the chief town of " the black country." Nowhere are the defects of our health laws more clearly or succinctly pointed out than in his letter to Sir George Grey, dated 15th Sept., 1865, and printed nearly entire by Mr. Hole in the appendix to his work.* And with a view to the removal of the nuisances which abound in Wolverhampton, and the adoption of comprehensive measures of sanitary reform, a searching inquiry is about to be instituted (6th Oct., 1866), " through the aid of a staff of gentlemen visitors, in order to procure a ' sanitary house-to-house return' upon the important questions of overcrowding, water-supply, drainage, ventilation, and other matters." The schedule printed for the use of the visitors is so complete and so in-structive a document, that I would fain have availed myself of the per-mission spontaneously given me by Mr. Hayes, and reprinted it for the guidance of those who elsewhere are endeavouring to promote the health and wellbeing of their respective neighbourhoods.

I am indebted to my friend Dr. Fleming, of Birmingham, for a copy of the *Birmingham Daily Post* (June 21, 1866), which contains a most valuable and striking article on the death-rate in the various towns of the black country, and enables me to add some informa-tion, which I had almost despaired of obtaining, regarding their sanitary condition. If this, the ninth of the series, be a sample of the other articles, I would earnestly suggest their publication in a separate form, as an important contribution to our public health literature. " Here," writes the reporter, "is the average death-rate of the several towns named, for the years 1851-60, with their mean population and gross mortality." I add another column, shewing which of them have, and which have not, officers of health.

---

* " Homes of the Working Classes, pp. 190, 195."

	Officer of Health ?	Population.	Deaths.	Ten Years' average Death-rate per 1,000 living.
Wolverhampton	Yes.	52,442	16,195	30·88
Dudley	No.	41,468	10,999	26 52
West Bromwich	No.	38,193	10,421	27·28
Tipton	Yes.	26,871	7,183	26·73
Walsall	No.	25,804	6,713	26·01
Bilston	No.	23,945	7,311	30·53
Willenhall	No.	21,299	5,663	26·58
Wednesbury	Yes.	18,124	4,628	25 53
Oldbury	Yes.	15,118	4,091	27·06
Darlaston	No.	12,100	3,672	30·34

England and Wales	22·24
Birmingham	24·90
These ten Towns..	27·74

One or two remarks in reference to this table. There was no officer of health in Wolverhampton when this account of these towns was published ; and here is the report of Oldbury :—" It is in a filthy condition—has no sewerage, keeps pigs, hugs a pestilential brook, and empties its privies into. public places. *It has a medical officer of health, whom it is trying*, after a nine months' trial, *to get rid of.*" West Bromwich "has a bad supply of water, has not yet banished pigs; and *it buries its dead in the centre of the town !*" Bilston, famous in the annals of the cholera, both in 1832 and 1849, has now a death-rate " within a fraction as large as that of Wolverhampton, exceeding West Bromwich by three, Dudley by four, and all England by eight. Its lower quarters reek with abominations." "Tipton is the·model town of the Black Country. It is naturally the worst situated for health in the whole district. Yet its death-rate exceeds Dudley only by a few hundredths. The reason is that it has a complete system of deep sewerage and a medical officer of health, and is wonderfully well looked after sanitarily." As regards the populations, again, the numbers, it will be seen, vary very remarkably in the different tables. Thus, in Table II, group A, the population of Wolverhampton is stated, according to the Municipal Corporations' Directory, at 63,985 in 1866 ; whereas it is stated by the Birmingham reporter as 52,442 ; and in the table from the General Register Office (Table IV.) as 126,902. This last, as explained in the *Daily Post,* " deals only with registrars' districts." What appears as Wolverhampton includes—besides the town of Wolverhampton— Bilston, Willenhall, Wombourn, Kinfare, and Tettenhall; in-cluding, doubtless, " a larger proportion of healthily than of un-healthily-housed population." It appears, however, from the small death-rate for the five years 1860-65, in the Somerset House Table IV., that there has been a marked improvement during that period over the whole registration district, though, in the absence of the returns from the sub-districts, we cannot tell where that improvement has been greatest.

This writer's summary of results gives in few words a striking picture of the actual condition of this important cluster of towns. "But taking the Birmingham average (24·90) for the black country towns, and adding the three lives already arrived at," (by allowing a larger mortality for the much larger population of Birmingham,) " it would appear that ten persons in every thousand of the inhabitants of these towns, die from preventable causes. Nor is this to be wondered at, when we consider that only three of them (including Walsall) have any system of sewerage : that only a like number have a medical officer of health ; that only one (Tipton) has both ; and that as to one of those which have a system of sewerage (Bilston), the town is shamefully neglected. It seems a dreadful thing to contemplate that, while the black country towns are on the whole healthily situated, and while their trades are not in the main injurious to health, their death-rate should still furnish something like *five* per thousand to swell the general rate of the rural districts, which stand at something like 18." Dr. Julian Hunter mentions,* as an indication of good intentions, that " the byelaws of Dudley provide for the duties of an officer of health, should one be appointed," and that " the duties are described at considerable length." Of Swansea also he reports (p. 189) that, " they had formerly the services of an officer of health, but on his resignation some years ago, the appointment was not filled up. The services of this officer were much valued, and regret was expressed by some of the inhabitants that the office had been abolished." †

The aggregate yearly amount expended in payment of medical officers of health by the 18 towns in group B., with their 2,057,561 inhabitants is £3,612 12s. giving an average salary of £190 2s. 9d. But, as £2,350—or nearly two-thirds of the total amount—is made up of the salaries of *four* of the nineteen, there remains to be divided among the other fifteen £1,262 12s. which gives an average of £83 3s. 3d.! Or if we deduct £2,750, which represents the salaries of *six* of the nineteen, the remaining thirteen have a miserable

---

* Eighth Report, &c., p. 131.

† In answer to inquiries recently made, (April 1867), I find that Oxford, Reading, and Wolverhampton have all discharged their officers of health ; Maidstone, I believe, has done likewise : Lincoln alone retains her medical adviser, but without a fixed salary, preferring to pay him by the job, or as they more euphoniously put it, according to work done by him ! So then we have medical officers of health in 19 out of 59, or, if we add the other nine black country towns, in 22 out of 68 large towns in England, Wales, and Scotland. I find also that, owing to the illness of the gentleman who undertook the organization of a staff of visitors, the house to house visitation in Wolverhampton has been delayed, though not abandoned.

residuum of £862 12s. to be divided among them, giving to each an average salary of £66 13s. 8d. But this is not the whole truth, for the variations are much greater than in the metropolitan district. On the one hand, the good town of Aberdare is not ashamed to offer twelve guineas annually, which means five shillings a week, or eight pence halfpenny a day, for looking after the health of 35,000 inhabitants. Nor does Paisley blush to give £20, or seven shillings and eight pence of weekly pay, for attending to the sanitary interests of 48,000. On the other hand, Liverpool has shown that it appreciates and knows how to reward ability of the highest order, by lately increasing Dr. Trench's salary from £750 to £1000 per annum. It would be interesting to know which of these masters is the more exacting. Most likely, judging from ordinary experience, those who reward their faithful servants with half the pay of a common day-labourer. Alongside of these beggarly allowances, let me place the following extracts as to "the duties and qualifications of officers of health," from the "Instructional Minute of the General Board of Health," dated December 20th, 1855 :—

"He will make himself familiar with the natural and acquired features of the place, with the social and previous sanitary state of its population, and with all its existing provisions for health;— viz., with the levels, inclinations, soil, wells, and watersprings of the district; with its meteorological peculiarities; with the distribution of its buildings and open spaces, paved or unpaved, of its burial grounds and lay stalls; with the plan of its drains, sewers, and water-supply; with the nature of its manufacturing and other industrial establishments; with the house-accommodation of the poorer classes, and the facilities afforded them for bathing and washing; with the arrangements for the burial of the dead; and with the regulations in force for lodging-houses and slaughtering-places, for the cleansing of public ways and markets, and for the removal of domestic refuse. * * * He will invite communications relating to the sanitary wants of the district, * * * take the best means in his power to become acquainted from week to week, and, in times of severe disease, from day to day, with the deaths and sicknesses in his district; and he will inquire to what extent they have depended on removable causes. With the assistance of such officers as the Local Board may empower him to direct and superintend, he will without intermission see to the wholesomeness of his district; * * * inquire as to the cleanly, wholesome, and weatherproof condition of houses; * * * examine from time to time the drinking-waters of the place, and observe whether provisions are offered for sale in any damaged and adulterated state that is hurtful or illegal. He will occasionally visit all burial-places, * * * and will habitually observe the slaughtering-houses of the district, and other industrial establishments which are liable to emit offensive (especially animal) effluvia. He will report to the Local Board weekly, annually, and at such intervening times as may require it."

"For the proper performance of these duties, special qualifications in science are required. These lie in pathology, including vital statistics, and in chemistry, with natural philosophy :—

" in *pathology*, because this science implies an exact study of the causes of disease in their relation to the living body,—a study of what they are, and how they act, and why they seem to vary in operation :

" in *vital statistics* (properly a section of pathology), because, by analysing the composition of various death-rates, and by learning how the pressure of particular diseases differs under different circumstances of climate, season, dwelling, age, sex, and occupation, definite standards of comparison are gained, without which the officer of health could not estimate the healthiness or unhealthiness of the population under his charge :

" in *chemistry* (including the power of microscopical observation) because without such aid there can be no accurate judgment as to impurities of air and water, dangerous impregnations of soil, or poisonous admixtures in food * * * :

" in *natural philosophy*, because many nuisances are traced, and many questions as to ventilation and over-crowding are answered by its laws; further, because by its aid the officer of health studies the atmospheric changes, and learns the climate of his district—important steps in proceeding to speak of its diseases; and finally, because natural philosophy in conjunction with chemistry renders him competent to report on many manufacturing processes alleged to be hurtful to health, and on the sufficiency of such means as are employed to reduce the evils ascribed to them."

And all these accomplishments—embracing more than half the circle of the sciences—for five shillings, or seven-and-eightpence a-week ! "Admirable Crichtons," it would seem, are to be had cheap nowadays. But Aberdare and Paisley at all events allow their officers of health to engage in private practice, and, by the salaries which they give them, virtually tell them that their sanitary duties need not occupy more than a fraction of their time. It is not always thus—witness Southampton. The story of the sanitary achievements of this prosperous and rapidly-growing seaport is far too instructive to be dismissed with a passing allusion. Southampton was one of the first (having been anticipated only by Liverpool and Leicester) to appoint a medical officer of health—the office having been instituted in 1850, when that admirable and much enduring public servant, Mr. Francis Cooper, was chosen as officer of health and sanitary inspector (the latter being the genteel designation of an inspector of nuisances), with the modest yearly salary of £150. Most likely he would not have undertaken such laborious duties for so inadequate a remuneration, had he not been permitted to devote to private practice the remnants of time that were not absorbed by official engagements. If so, he was not long of discovering how incompatible with private practice was the fearless denunciation of abominations, in the maintenance of which some of his employers in the Town Council had a vested interest ; and at length, in the ruin of his practice, which might possibly have been improved by a judicious reticence, he found how expensive it is to keep a conscience. And if, at the outset, he expected that a zealous discharge of his duties would soon secure for him an increase of salary, he must have been cruelly disappointed, for it was not till he had toiled for thirteen years, that his salary was raised to £200. In the autumn of 1865, as all the world knows, Southampton was visited with "an outbreak of cholera, and" I quote Dr. Wiblin's words, "poor Cooper's great energies were taxed beyond endurance. He was called to every form of nuisance that existed in the town; he had to appear before magistrates to give evidence to prove that stinks and abominations did actually prevail, although neither he nor they could remove the most formidable and pestiferous privy abominations which abound here. Borne down by the multiplicity of his duties, and the want of support in carrying them out," he quickly succumbed to an attack of the pestilence, the further spread of which he was resolutely striving to prevent. A clear official homicide; after perpetrating which the Council met and passed a resolution of condolence, which was duly forwarded to his bereaved and sorrowing family. I have not called it a murder, for it was done in ignorance and not with intent to kill; but the ignorance was such as should be accounted criminal; and the heartless treatment that led to the untimely death of so valuable a public officer not only verifies the maxim that "corporate bodies have no conscience," but shows most strikingly the need of an efficient check on the wrongheadedness and parsimony of local authorities. The concluding sentence of Dr. Julian Hunter's report on Southampton * addresses itself to us like a voice from Francis Cooper's grave, and embodies the matured experience of a man who was worried to death in the conscientious discharge of the duties of an underpaid and thankless office. "The inconvenience," writes Dr. H., "of combining the prosecution of nuisances with private medical practice, as indeed with any private business at all, was almost daily apparent, and Mr. Cooper thought better results would be got by a combination of towns to support a medical officer who should have no other engagement, and who would be entirely free from local influences." How was the lesson improved by the Town Council?

During the prevalence of the epidemic, not only were the Sanitary Committee unbounded in their liberality, and profuse in their expenditure, both on the medical attendants and on those smitten with the pestilence, but the Mayor (Mr. Emanuel) and Mr. Alderman Stebbing were unwearied in their personal efforts, visiting from house to house during sixteen or seventeen hours of the twenty-four, administering to the wants and comforts of the sick, and solacing the inhabitants of the most suffering districts. Then came the question of appointing a successor to Mr. Cooper. It was resolved to separate the offices of Officer of Health and Inspector of Nuisances, and to advertise for a gentleman to fill the first office, who should be debarred from private

---

* Eighth Report of the Medical Officer of the Privy Council. Appendix, p. 184.

practice, and receive the annual salary of £150! It will scarcely be believed that the post has been accepted on these terms by a highly educated and accomplished gentleman, who is thoroughly up to his work, and discharges his duties (his detractors themselves being witnesses) with singular ability. At the same time, as if in studied and bitter mockery of the medical and other learned professions, the council appointed, as inspector of nuisances, with a salary of £100 a year, " a man without education or any special qualification, and quite independent of the officer of health." If Dr. MacCormack has no respect for himself and for the profession to which he belongs, if he courts a repetition of the insults to which he has been subjected by the Town Council, and if he covets the melancholy fate of his lamented predecessor, he will retain, on its present footing, the menial office he has so injudiciously accepted. Let us note, however, that the mortality of Southampton (see Table IV.), which had increased from 23 to 24 per 1,000 between 1850 and 1861, has declined to 21 per 1,000 during the five years 1860-65. But there is no reason why, with its advantages of situation, it should not show even a lower death-rate.

Happily there is another side to the picture. There are towns scattered here and there throughout the kingdom, in which much has been done by the civic authorities to improve the public health. I need not refer to Croydon, which has been so often mentioned of late years as a model in its sanitary arrangements, except to express my surprise that it has no officer of health. Those who wish for detailed information will find it in an interesting pamphlet, in which my friend, Dr. Westall, has published the results of his ten years' experience as a member of the Local Board of Health*. Nor can I say anything of what has been accomplished in Coventry, Huddersfield, Leek, and Macclesfield, in all of which, especially in Leek, the improvement has been very palpable, as I know of no correspondent to whom I can address myself in these and in many other towns. My space forbids me to do more than supplement the statements of my table by a few brief notices of special circumstances connected with some of the towns enumerated in it.

It will be observed that only *four* towns besides Southampton have engaged officers of health for sanitary work alone. Birkenhead gives £350, Edinburgh and Leeds £500, and Liverpool £1,000 of annual salary. Birkenhead will probably find it a judicious economy to give a more liberal allowance : for though the Sanitary Committee have found, in Dr. Baylis, an able successor to Dr. Robinson made ready to their hands, they may learn, as the demand for health officers becomes greater, that Birkenhead is but a training-school for the rest of England. "In Birkenhead," writes Dr. Robinson, "the authorities delegate to their medical officer of health full power to

---

* " The advantages to be derived from the adoption of the Local Government Act, as exemplified in Croydon." Ridgway, London, 1865.

act according to his judgment, an advantage of no small moment; for when municipal bodies cripple and thwart their health-officer, his usefulness is seriously undermined and curtailed." I shall speak presently of Dr. Robinson's experience in Leeds.

In the city of millionaires across the Mersey, with its frightful death-rate which has attracted so much attention of late years, the officer of health is and has long been one of the most important of its public men. The respect due both to the late Dr. Duncan and to Dr. Trench for their own high qualities has been naturally enhanced by the signal services they have rendered, in a town where so many of the producing causes of deadly epidemics are at work with an activity and intensity unsurpassed—if even parallelled—in any other town of the United Kingdom. The officer of health is there not only a reality, but a power in the commonwealth. . I do not mean to assert that all has been done that might have been done—very far from it—or that the sanitary committee have adopted and carried out all the recommendations of Dr. Trench and his eminent predecessor, and of their zealous fellow-workers, Mr. Newlands, the borough engineer, and Mr. McGowen, the late town clerk, whose loss to Liverpool cannot but be a great gain to Bradford. But the officer of health is in Liverpool recognised by the civic authorities as their official adviser, whose opinion is asked and listened to with deference in all matters relating to the public health; and having proved himself worthy of their confidence, he has been entrusted by them with very large discretionary powers, which he has exercised with great tact and judgment in furtherance of the views of the health committee and the provisions of the sanitary Acts. The problem of the excessive death-rate of Liverpool* is one which concerns the whole nation, and which has been carefully investigated by the "mortality sub-committee," whose report, and the evidence on which it is founded, form one of the most instructive and painfully-interesting volumes that has appeared for many years. " The result of the inquiry (Report, p. ix) is the conviction, supported by a mass of evidence, that the proximate causes of the increased death-rate are intemperance, indigence, and overcrowding; these two latter being generally found in the train of intemperance, although all three act and re-act on each other as cause and effect. . . . . The evidence abundantly shows that the vice (intemperance) is alarmingly prevalent among the labouring population, and that its wretched victims and their families sink rapidly into squalid poverty, resulting in overcrowding and its attendant evils. Liverpool has also this peculiarity, that it has a greater amount of unskilled labourers in proportion to its population than any other

---

* In the table furnished by Dr. Farr (Table IV.), we find the following figures:—

Death Rate per 1000 living :—

	1841—50.	1851—60.	1861—65.
Liverpool	36	33	36
West Derby	26	23	26

town, for whom employment is uncertain and wages small and irregular." It should also be remembered that multitudes of its comfortable and opulent citizens reside not only out of Liverpool, but out of Lancashire, thus greatly diminishing in Liverpool the proportion of the class among whom the death-rate is smallest, and greatly lessening the death-rate of Birkenhead, Claughton, Oxton, Egremont, New Brighton, &c. I insist very strongly on these important facts, because I have been asked, with an air of triumph— What is the use of your medical officer of health, when, in spite of him, you have such a death-rate? Just so; it *is* in spite of him; but without him, thoughtful men will be disposed to inquire, might not the twenty-five years' average have been forty-five instead of thirty-five? The resolution adopted by the corporation, in accordance with the recommendations of the sub-committee, to spend £250,000 in " breaking up the masses of crowded dwellings by driving thoroughfares through and across them to let in the light and the air," and so to encourage the construction of decent dwellings for the labouring classes, shows a disposition to follow the example set on a much larger scale by the Glasgow authorities, and cannot fail to influence beneficially the health of their constituents.

Dr. Littlejohn occupies in Edinburgh a position exactly corresponding to that of Dr. Trench in Liverpool, and meets with hearty co-operation on the part of the authorities in all his endeavours to improve the sanitary condition of the city, the death-rate of which was in 1859 as low as 21·09, and in 1862 as high as 26·65, the average for five years being 24·15 per 1,000. The advantage of having officers of health set apart exclusively for sanitary work is very manifest in the reports of Dr. Trench and Dr. Littlejohn, which embrace not only the chief causes of excessive mortality, but the death-rate of different ages, seasons, districts, and even streets, indicating the chief haunts of so-called " zymotic " diseases and the measures most likely to be useful in lessening the preventible mortality. It is quite clear that very few gentlemen largely engaged in private practice can command the leisure necessary for fully recording their sanitary experience, and deducing the lessons to be derived therefrom. In his paper " On the Cleansing Operations of Edinburgh," read before the Social Science Association in 1863,* Dr. Littlejohn gives an interesting account of the system which has been in use since 1839, for the immediate removal of all solid refuse, not only from the streets but from all the houses. The inspector of cleansing has under him eight district overseers or assistant inspectors, and 135 scavengers, each of whom has his own beat. The old town and the poorer districts of the new are visited twice, but the greater portion of the new town only once a day; so that " all accumulations of filth are thus prevented for a longer period than a few hours, and the refuse thus collected is sold as manure, so as to yield a revenue to

---

* *Soc. Sc. Transactions*, 1863, p. 513.

the city." " This mode of cleansing, which needs only the simplest machinery, puts £7,000 per annum into the local treasury," and " from a report presented to the Town Council in 1859, it appears that from Whitsunday 1839 to Whitsunday 1859—a period of twenty years—830,000 tons of solid refuse were collected from the streets and sold for £158,000."

Those who have perused my quotations regarding the condition of Leeds do not need to be informed that Dr. Robinson, in repairing thither from Birkenhead, undertook a task of no ordinary magnitude; and most men would have recoiled from the prospect of grappling with unparellelled privy abominations, piggeries by hundreds, noisome slaughter houses, the gigantic smoke nuisance, and an average death-rate of 30 in the 1,000. The work has been bravely begun, and the incidents of the struggle will be historic. The long-denounced piggeries were selected as the battle-ground, and Leeds was for some time convulsed with the mighty strife! We have all heard of "learned pigs," but it was reserved for the West Riding of Yorkshire to bring to light in 1866 the new portent of political pigs. Thoroughly alarmed by the decisive blow aimed by Dr. Robinson at their vested rights, the pig-owners of Leeds, with the double view of averting their impending fate, and of turning the tables upon their adversary, formed themselves into a " Pig Protection Society," summoned indignation ward-meetings—at some of which members of the Town Council declaimed in favour of this form of liberty of the subject— and commenced an active canvass for the purpose of turning out from the council all who would not pledge themselves to vote for the dismissal of Dr. Robinson. And when the case came before the sitting magistrates, there was not wanting high medical testimony in favour of the salubrity of pigstyes, for my friend Mr. Nunneley " defied any person to say that the pig was worse than any other animal, and he believed that if it was kept clean it was no greater nuisance than a man. He kept a pig upon his own midden for sanitary purposes, and if anybody would try the experiment, they would find it to be a benefit, as he did." After this opinion—backed by that of Mr. Jessop, who considered that the effluvia from a pig were not more injurious than those from a human being—little wonder that another witness reached the climax by declaring that, after three years' experience, " he believed the effluvia to be more beneficial than otherwise!" Nevertheless, the magistrates, after a second hearing, found that pigs could not be kept in a town without being a nuisance, and a source of injury to the public health, and ordered their removal. The Recorder, however, before whom the cases were brought by appeal, gave an order, not for the eviction of the pigs, but for the daily removal of the manure, for the full enforcement of which a separate inspector would be required for every pigsty. Still the result has been the extermination of many from objectionable localities, and a great improvement in those which remain. Thus far " the crusade against the pigs."

In three particulars the officers of health in Leicester, Bristol, and Glasgow agree. They are not required to give up the whole of their time to their sanitary duties; they are all zealous, able, and thoroughly efficient; and they all receive miserably inadequate salaries. Mr. Moore, who has served Leicester faithfully and well for above seventeen years, has £100, and Mr. Davies and Professor Gairdner have each £200 a year. But the authorities, if they pay their officers shabbily, give them their confidence and support in the execution of their arduous and often invidious functions. Mr. Davies holds his appointment, which is a temporary one, under the Town Council as the Board of Health for Bristol, and was chosen by its health committee, who call him their " medical inspector," as they " object to the appointment of a medical officer under the Act." So thorough is the confidence reposed in him, that he has received no instructions, and is allowed to do his work in his own way; any point requiring a professional opinion is referred to him; and the magistrates shew every disposition to forward the views of the health committee and their officer, when proceedings are taken. That these have been often instituted since Mr. Davies's appointment, during the epidemic of typhus in February 1865, will appear from the following instructive extract. "A temporary fever hospital having been erected by voluntary contributions, I insisted on the removal of every typhus patient, or his isolation in such a manner as not to be dangerous to the health of others. All infected rooms were fumigated with chlorine by men under my direction. All infected clothing was destroyed. All privies in the infected district were flushed and disinfected with chloride of lime. New privies ordered to be erected where necessary, only two houses being allowed to use one privy. Every person removing from an infected house was watched for a considerable period. In three months typhus in its epidemic form was eradicated. It was originally introduced here from Ireland in April, 1864. All defective drains were remedied, dirty houses informed against, and cleansed at the expense of the landlords. All pigs that we could find were removed from the city by notice, or where necessary by proceedings before the magistrates. Cases of overcrowding were reported. Nuisances arising from manufactories where injurious to health have been proceeded against, but *much remains* to be done under this head." Mr. Davies's italics shew that on this point he is at one with a writer in the *Quarterly Journal of Science* for October 1866, though he justly complains of the selection (in an article in the number for July) of the mortality returns for a single week in March, when, owing to the extensive prevalence of measles, whooping-cough, and capillary bronchitis, the death-rate of Bristol rose to 40 in the 1,000 : a sensational artifice unworthy of a writer in a scientific journal. The truth is, as the writer admits in his October article, that while the death-rate of some very poor and overcrowded localities in the Hotwell Road and the neighbourhood of the basins is high, that of Bristol generally is very moderate, while Clifton is often as low as 6 or 7 in the 1,000. It will be seen from Table IV. that Bristol is one of those towns which exhibit a steadily decreasing death-rate during the last 25 years, while that of Clifton is rather on the increase.*

Still, beyond a doubt, Bristol neither looks nor smells wholesome. The odours that greet the stranger on his arrival, or while walking the streets, from all sorts of factories, but especially from slaughter-houses, tanneries, bone-boiling and tallow-chandlers' establishments, and from the fœtid waters of the floating harbour, give evidence the reverse of welcome how much room there is for improvement. Mr. Davies does his part by keeping a daily journal of his own work, which is read every week to the health committee; and by meeting his inspectors every morning to receive their reports and give his instructions. What he has done for the prevention of the spread of cholera, and with what signal success, is well known in Bristol through the public prints, and by the rest of the world through the deeply interesting article of Dr. W. Budd on "The Asiatic Cholera in Bristol in 1866."† Those who know how abundant are his labours and how great his expenditure of time, will more than share his doubts whether he—though assuredly Bristol—is a gainer by his tenure of office on the present terms. His fellow-workers of "The Sanitary Mission," Mrs. Norris and her companions, of whose unwearied exertions during the presence of the cholera he has sent me—and Dr. Budd has also given—a most interesting account, deserve the warmest thanks of their fellow-citizens, and the imitation of others throughout the country.

It is pleasing to know that in Glasgow a similar spirit manifested itself, and under the guidance of Dr. Gairdner has been turned to good account, in prospect of a visit of the cholera, and that hundreds have offered themselves for the work of house to house visitation. Glasgow differs from all the other towns of which I have spoken, in having one principal medical officer of health, and under him four district medical officers (one of whom is surgeon to the police force) as medical assistants or inspectors, who do not receive fixed salaries, but are paid according to the services required of them. Dr. Gairdner informs me that this arrangement answers well, as these gentlemen have an intimate knowledge of the diseases prevalent, and especially of the fever haunts, in the districts of which they have the oversight. Their employment under the health officer is a happy instance of the adaptation of a useful agency, which had been long in existence, to our modern sanitary requirements. Dr. Gairdner, occupying as he does a position of great eminence among scientific men, is naturally consulted and listened to with great deference by the enlightened authorities of the commercial metropolis in Scotland, and may almost be said to wield at will its great resources for the reduction of its very high death-rate; for the eradication, if that be possible, of the endemic typhus, which so often bursts into sweeping epidemics that carry off thousands of yearly victims; and for the radical reform of the loath-

---

* See p. 48.
† *British Medical Journal*, April 13, 1867.

some wynds and vennals where that indigenous pestilence is bred and perpetuated. For the purpose of improving out of existence these proverbial plague-spots, the authorities have obtained an Act of Parliament, * which " extends over ten years," and enables them to expend £1,250,000 in the purchase of bad property, after the removal of which the ground will be disposed of and new buildings erected, under the admirable provisions of the Police and Improvement Act. An example worthy of imitation by Manchester and other large towns, where the accommodation for multitudes of the labouring-classes is of the worst description. The account drawn up by Dr. Gairdner † of the visit he paid, along with the Lord Provost, Baillie Raeburn, and Mr. Carrick to Paris, in June 1866, is full of interesting and suggestive materials bearing on the reconstruction and proper regulation of large towns. Another document of great public interest, and a most important contribution to our "fever literature," is the Report, ‡ by Dr. Russell, of the City Fever Hospital, which was constructed on the most approved plan under the eye of Dr. Gairdner. It embraces many valuable suggestions on diet, nursing, construction, arrangement and ventilation of hospital buildings, treatment of patients, and management of convalescents, besides a thorough analysis of the statistical results. The growing filthiness, however, of the noble river, which is one of the great sources of the wealth of Glasgow, is a standing menace to the health and lives of the vast and rapidly increasing population that lines its banks, and an offensive nuisance for many miles of its seaward course.

Dr. Julian Hunter, in his report on Cardiff, § remarks that "Dr. Paine has the confidence both of the poor people and of the bench of magistrates, so much that the first seldom require anything more than his advice to move them to whatever is necessary, and the latter are disposed to accept his opinion as conclusive on all health matters which come before them." This wise and prudent counsellor has received £40 a year (in all £520) for the invaluable services he has rendered to the 33,000 inhabitants of Cardiff since 1853. Dr. Davies, (Newport,) is paid, as he justly remarks, "less than any inspector of nuisances," and for the miserable salary of £50 he visits overcrowded houses and lodging-houses, examines unwholesome food and meat, "gives medical attendance to the police, and attends to the ordinary duties very much to the satisfaction of the authorities." ‖ Mr. Dyke has commenced his duties with exemplary ability and zeal, for £60 a

---

* Glasgow City Improvement Act.

† Notes of Personal Observations and Inquiry in June, 1866, on the City Improvements of Paris, &c. Presented to the Magistrates, &c., of the City of Glasgow, 2nd October, 1866.

‡ Report of the City of Glasgow Fever Hospital, from 25th April, 1865, to 30th April, 1866. By Dr. James B. Russell, Physician and Superintendent. Presented to the Magistrates' Committee of the Board of Police, by Dr. Gairdner, and ordered to be printed, 16th August, 1866.

§ Eighth Report, &c., p. 123.

‖ Eighth Report, &c., p. 158.

year. Mr. Barter's services are valued by the corporation of Bath at £25 more than those of the borough inspector; and Mr. Fairbank, after two years of conscientious and very efficient labour, finds that his practice has suffered by his accepting the appointment of officer of health for Doncaster.

Have I not adduced sufficient evidence to establish the necessity of a government check on the appointment, remuneration, and dismissal of officers of health, and the expediency, both for their own interests and for those of the public, of making them independent alike of local caprice and of private practice? But if the need of a central authority to regulate the action of not a few of those who have availed themselves of the permission to institute that office be great, how much greater the need of legislative interference to enjoin the appointment of health officers on those who construe the Act as giving permission *not* to appoint them. Fully alive as I am to the force of Mr. Rumsey's arguments* against having officers of health for small districts, and to the difficulties in the way of a satisfactory adjustment of many small towns and country districts with scattered populations, I cannot see that either the arguments or the difficulties apply to towns with populations of 30,000 and upwards. I do not see why parliament should not at once empower the Privy Council to enjoin their appointment in all such cases, reserving for future decision the question of enlarging the districts by including outlying smaller towns, or neighbouring country parishes, where such a measure might seem desirable. In many cases the registration districts might be at once adopted; and the longer I consider the subject, the more am I inclined to accept Mr. Rumsey's suggestion, that " registration districts are the best areas for local sanitary administration," as promising the most satisfactory solution of this difficult problem.

Of the 36 towns which have no officers of health (Table III.), in only 11 is the population under 30,000, while in 25 it ranges from 31,000 to above 380,000, thus:—

Under 20,000 ...	...	...	...	...	6
Above 20,000 and under 30,000			...	...	5
„ 30,000	„	50,000	...	...	10
„ 50,000	„	100,000	...	...	7
„ 100,000	„	200,000	...	...	5
„ 200,000 ...	...	...	...	...	3
					36

Birmingham and Manchester being two of the last three, with populations respectively of 338,868 and 380,887. In Aberdeen " a medical officer of health should have been appointed some time ago, with a salary of £200 a year, but from some differences between the

---

* " Comments on the Sanitary Act, 1866," &c. Reprinted from *Journal of Social Science* for October, 1866.

candidates it has been postponed, Dr. Ogston being temporarily appointed." In Birmingham, the assistance of the able borough analyst (Dr. Alfred Hill) is occasionally called in by the Borough Inspection Committee. In Cambridge, the appointment of a health officer has been strongly urged on the sanitary committee, but the proposition did not meet with favour. In Cheltenham, the appointment has been negatived, chiefly on the plea that it would frighten the public. As regards Derby, Dr. Ogle thinks " that perhaps the sort of work that is already being done (house to house visitation and isolation of infectious cases) is as much as the people would submit to, and that it is almost better not to have a health officer until the public feel the necessity more, and would be willing to pay him better. Looking ahead to the time when such officers will be considered at least as necessary to the public *body* as a solicitor is to protect the public *property*, would it not be well that such a one should be the registrar, and the vaccinator" (*query*, the inspector of vaccination?), "and that returns of disease, at any rate from parochial medical officers, should be sent to him?" Devonport has "only just (October, 1866) accepted the Local Government Act, many of the most important provisions of which will no doubt be enforced in the course of the next twelvemonth." In Exeter, fears are expressed—and probably with justice if he were entirely dependent on the local authorities—that he would be under the pressure of the trading classes. In Gloucester, " local prejudices prove too great obstacles." In Hull, some of the parochial medical officers are occasionally employed by the guardians as medical inspectors of nuisances; but there is no proper sanitary organization of the town, which seems (from Table IV.) to be losing the high reputation it gained under the enlightened and active mayoralty of Mr. (now Sir Henry) Cooper, as the death-rate has risen during the last five years, in Hull from 25 to 26, and in Sculcoates from 22 to 24. The authorities in Manchester not only doggedly resist, but actively oppose the appointment of a health officer, and the adoption of other measures calculated to improve the sanitary state of the town. In Northampton, " the matter has been urged on the town authorities, but owing to a false economy nothing has been done." In Nottingham, the inspector, who is a valuable officer and does his work well, naturally considers and represents as needless an officer whose appointment would render his position less important, and diminish his salary. " The town council," writes Dr. Hall (September 25, 1866), " of a town like Sheffield, with 210,000 inhabitants, not having appointed an officer of health is matter of regret. All large towns ought to be obliged to appoint such an officer. Sheffield has not been so healthy for years as during the last four months. The death-rate has been (on an average each month) abont 22 to 24 to each 1000, instead of 32 to 34, as it was last year. I attribute this in a great measure to the constant heavy rains having kept our drains and water courses free from filth. It is contemplated to keep our sewage out of our rivers." A reference to Table IV, shows a steadily increasing death-rate in Sheffield itself, and for Ecclesale Bierlow, a recent decrease from 23 to 21 per 1000. In Tynemouth the authorities "have been deterred by the expense," and in York, says Mr. Husband, "the corporation have long been talking of appointing a medical officer of health, but have made talking serve." With such a situation and great capabilities of improvement, the death-rate of York should not exceed 19 or 20 in the 1000. Mr. Husband, after referring to the Leeds pig battle, asks the pertinent question, "Does not this shew that the medical officer of health should be appointed by Government, and be thus independent of the ratepayers who court the nuisances?" I have reserved Stafford till the last, for the purpose of giving the subjoined companion pictures, in illustration of its sanitary progress.

STAFFORD IN 1849.	STAFFORD IN 1866.
"In that town, as I learn through the kindness of Dr. Harland, there is not a single sewer, and the liquid refuse from the houses runs down the channels on each side of the streets. It is common at the poorer houses to have holes dug in the ground to allow the waste and refuse water and drain into it. The town is built on a bed of sand, and water is everywhere found at 8 to 10 feet below the surface, and the whole of the inhabitants have pumps convenient to their dwellings. Dr. Harland says he has no doubt that in many cases the refuse liquid must percolate through the sand and get into the pump water, and he has known some instances in which the filthy surface-water was allowed to get into the wells." Dr. Snow, *Med. Gazette,* N. S., vol. ix. 1849, p. 926.	"The sanitary condition of Stafford is so little thought of, and all the arrangements connected therewith are so primitive and imperfect, that, without referring to any one else, I can give you all the information you seek for. First, there is no officer of health, and only one inspector of nuisances. Until very recently, this officer was a policeman; *now,* a man who is a cooper and collector of rates is employed, and he is said to discharge his duties in a very *in*efficient manner. The drainage is all on the surface, and the odour therefrom, at times, disgustingly offensive. The water supply of the whole town is obtained from wells, many of them in close proximity to receptacles of filth; and I am in the habit of saying, partly in joke, but principally in earnest, that the persons living at No. 6 drink the water that is *made* at No. 7."

As regards the lessons to be drawn from Table IV., I cannot enter on the deeply interesting subject of the relation between death-rate and density of population. With the materials before them, many of my readers will doubtless pursue that investigation for themselves. I can but present in the most striking and compendious form, as in the following triple list, the answer to the question, what progress has been made during the last quarter of a century?

In 18 districts, then, out of 58 included in Table IV., we have a decreasing death-rate. In eight, viz., Bristol, Cheltenham, Newport, Oxford, Plymouth, East Stonehouse, Stoke, and Portsea, the diminution, which is notable, has been going on over the whole period; while in ten it has taken place only during the last five years, having previously been either stationary or increasing. Four in the second column, viz., Aston (Birmingham), Maidstone, Newcastle, and York, have maintained throughout uniform average death-rates respectively of 21, 23, 27, and 24 in the 1,000. In eleven, though less than in

DEATH RATE.

Decreasing in 18 Districts, viz. :—	Stationary in 20 Districts, viz. :—	Increasing in 20 Districts, viz. ;—
Bristol.	*Aston.*	Clifton.
Cardiff.	** Bath.	Cambridge.
Cheltenham.	Birmingham.	Chester.
Chichester.	* Bradford.	Gloucester.
Derby.	* Brighton.	Grimsby.
Gateshead.	** Canterbury.	Halifax.
Merthyr Tydfil.	** Carlisle.	Hastings.
Newport (Monmouth.)	* Doncaster.	Headington.
Nottingham.	** Exeter.	{ Hull and
Oxford.	** Hereford.	{ Sculcoates.
{ Plymouth.	** King's Lynn.	Leeds.
{ East Stonehouse.	*Maidstone.*	Leicester.
{ Stoke Damerel.	** Manchester.	Lincoln.
Portsea Island.	*Newcastle-on-Tyne.*	{ Liverpool and
Ecclesale Bierlow.	Norwich.	{ West Derby.
Southampton.	** Reading.	Northampton.
Sunderland.	** Salford.	Sheffield.
Wolverhampton.	** Shrewsbury.	South Shields.
	** Tynemouth.	Stafford.
	York.	Worcester.

   * Higher than in 1841–50, since which stationary.
  ** Lower than in 1841–50, since which stationary.
    Those in *Italics* have been absolutely stationary since 1841.

the first ten, it has been stationary during the last fifteen years, at such rates as 21 (Hereford), 22 (Bath, King's Lynn, and Reading), 23 (Canterbury, Carlisle, and Tynemouth), 24 (Exeter), 25 (Shrewsbury), 26 (Salford), and 31 (Manchester); while in three, the death-rate of the last fifteen is higher than that of the first ten years. In four of the third column, viz., Grimsby, Halifax, Northampton, and Sheffield, the death-rate has been steadily increasing over the whole period ; while in the remaining sixteen the rise has taken place (in Leicester, Liverpool, and West Derby to a notable extent,) during the last five years.

    The general result, then, appears to be that in 18 out of 58 populous registration districts in England and Wales, the mortality is decreasing, while in 49 it is either stationary (in most cases at needlessly high rates) or increasing. But it must always be borne in mind that the mortality of the registration districts does not give us that of the sub-districts. In some instances, as in the case of Wolverhampton, already referred to, it may be too low ; in others, as in the case of Clifton, which is made responsible for the high mortality of "some of the poorest and densest portions of Bristol,"* much too

---

   * Dr. Edward Wilson's "Sanitary Statistics of Cheltenham," p. 45 ; also "The Sanitary Statistics of Clifton," by J. A. Symonds, M.D., F.R.S.E., *Transactions of British Association, &c.*, for 1864, p. 176.

high. One great advantage likely to flow from the appointment of highly qualified medical officers of health in all districts, rural as well as urban, would be the increased accuracy of our information in regard not only to the mortality, but to the diseases, both of districts and sub-districts throughout the country.

After the observations I made on the subject of inspection of nuisances in the Metropolitan districts, my remarks on Tables III. and V. shall be brief. The twenty-three towns in Table II. (to which Table V. is supplementary), with temporary or permanent officers of health, and an aggregate population of 2,220,407, have 103 ordinary inspectors or sub-inspectors, *i.e.* on an average one to 21,557 inhabitants. But if we deduct Leeds and Liverpool, their joint population of 710,085, and their staffs of inspectors amounting to 63, there remain only 40 for the other 21 towns, which have a population of 1,510,322, *i.e.* one inspector to 37,758; while Leeds has one to every 10,818, and Liverpool one to 11,498 inhabitants, exclusive of meat and common lodging-house inspectors. We must also remember that in Edinburgh, Glasgow, and Dundee, not only are there special market, slaughter-house and lodging-house inspectors, but the services of the police force, with all the local knowledge they possess, are at the command of the health officer and his men, when necessary. In all, except *six* of these towns, the inspection is reported as being either "efficient" or "very efficient," considering the small number generally employed, and the other duties which too often occupy their time and distract their attention from their sanitary work. In Bristol, for instance, Mr. Davies writes :—"I meet all the inspectors every morning at the office at 11 a.m. Through them I am daily informed of the state of the general health, &c., &c. They are taken as a rule from the detective constables, who are favourably known to the Watch Committee, many of whom are on the committee of the Board of Health. The only qualifications are ability to write a good hand, and a character for general shrewdness and integrity. They are all very able men, and know every body and everything in the city within their duties ; and so sharp that nothing escapes them. Being experienced detectives, each has his circle of informants. They work excessively hard, and are not numerous enough."

In the 36 towns in Table III., with an aggregate population of 2,601,165, (or deducting Salford, about which I have been unable to obtain any information, 2,489,760), there are 59 inspectors of nuisances, *i.e.* one to 42,200 inhabitants. I am aware that there is one inspector-in-chief for Manchester, but do not in the least know (though I have made repeated attempts to discover) the number of his staff of sub-inspectors. Rumour asserts that they are very far from efficient, and that nuisances of the most noisome kind are fostered, instead of being summarily put down, by the corporation. But we know from their admirable reports, that the members of the Sanitary Association have voluntarily and gratuitously carried out for many years, both in Manchester and Salford, a system of inspection and a registration of disease and mortality, of unequalled excellence—an example which ought to stimulate the authorities to a wholesome rivalry, but which seems rather to impress them with the idea that they are thereby relieved from all responsibility. If so, they need to be reminded, that to possess such information as is regularly furnished to them by the Sanitary Association, and not to act upon it, is to incur the responsibility and the guilt of wholesale homicide. If we allow 8 inspectors for Manchester and Salford, we shall then have 67 for the entire population of the 36 towns, *i.e.* one to 38,823 inhabitants. The metropolitan average, which we considered exceedingly defective, is one to 29,100. In 15 of the 36 the inspection is reported efficient, in four tolerably so, in eight doubtful or more than doubtful, and in four decidedly bad. It will be observed that, as in the metropolis, some of the inspectors have other duties to attend to, so that the inspection of nuisances is nearly or altogether nominal. Another point which calls for remark is the frequent employment of the police as sanitary inspectors. It is one thing to select men from the police force for their shrewdness, tact, and local knowledge, and to set them apart for sanitary work alone ; and quite another to make the inspection of nuisances a department of police. In the former plan, the one object in view is thoroughly efficient sanitary inspection by men highly qualified, and well remunerated, for that special work ; while the chief recommendation of the latter is probably the saving of expense. The services of the police are as a general rule underpaid, and their duties are sufficiently burthensome without the addition of a task which requires for its satisfactory performance the undivided energies of a separate staff. Besides, it is worthy of consideration, whether the identification of sanitary improvement with the force which is chiefly occupied in the prevention and repression of crime, is not calculated to prejudice the minds of many against the health-measures they are employed to put in execution.

The inspection of lodging-houses I have described in some instances (*e.g.*, Bristol and Bradford) as " indulgent." By this phrase I mean that, owing to the great want of proper accommodation for the labouring-classes, the authorities are reluctantly compelled to refrain from instituting proceedings against over-crowding, for fear—or rather from the certainty—of increasing the mischief in other quarters. I can do little more than indicate the evil, which, not in Bristol and Bradford only, but in the metropolis and in most of our large towns, is one of the chief hindrances to any effectual amelioration of the sanitary condition of the masses. In Manchester, the state of many of the registered lodging-houses is positively loathsome. One night, about ten o'clock, I sallied forth with several friends, under the protection of two police officers, and after spending nearly an hour in visiting the low public-houses, and mingling in the crowds of sots and desperadoes that filled them, we devoted a couple of hours to an inspection of a considerable number of lodging-houses. In all of them the atmosphere was foul and stifling, and in many the floors were so encrusted with dirt, that they seemed not to have been washed for months. In single room, six, eight, or ten beds, about two feet apart, contained as many couples, some of them of both sexes, and not unfrequently a close examination detected one or two little heads protruding from the foot of a bed, the rest of which was occupied by the parents. Some of the children—those, probably, who had not long breathed the polluted atmosphere of these dwellings—looked plump and fairly healthy; but we saw others vainly trying to extract sufficient nourishment from the shrivelled breasts of half-tipsy mothers, while their ghostlike frames, and weird, haggard looks that made one shudder, told a sickening tale of slow starvation, and of long years of suffering crowded into their few months of existence. In the dim light, we often stumbled over heaps of ragged garments swarming with all sorts of vermin, and found that in these police-inspected haunts, where water was as scarce as air, the personal filth was in perfect keeping with the moral pollution of the migratory inmates. One other picture I extract from a deeply interesting report (sent to me by Dr. Marshall) on "Workmen's Houses in Greenock." The following is a summary of a table of sanitary statistics obtained from a house to house visitation, conducted by working men in 1863. "Thirty-two persons are living in apartments having less than 50 cubic feet of air! A supply so scanty, that it is difficult to understand how suffocation does not follow. 542 persons have less than 100 cubic feet. 1,179 persons have under 150 cubic feet. 3,437 persons have under 450 cubic feet, living and sleeping in a condition actually dangerous to life. But the result by far the most appalling is this, that out of 3,749 persons whose cases have been examined, not a small proportion, not a-half, but *the whole*, with the insignificant deduction of 57 individuals, are living and sleeping in habitations in which health cannot be maintained, and in a state the inevitable result of which must be that the springs of life must dry up, and may perhaps entirely fail. This is not the worst of it. Seven hundred cubic feet of air is enough for a grown person, if it be pure; but if it has wandered into the room from between the high gables of back lands (*i.e.* tenements)—if it have passed over noxious ashpits, and over courts and entries destitute of sewerage; if it be already poisoned before it has filtered into the deadly crowded sleeping places, how much is the evil aggravated? Now, it is to be remembered that this is not the picture of the worst parts of Greenock, of dens of misery to which the rest of the dwellings form a contrast; but it is the worst and the best taken together, where working men dwell. It is a faithful picture of how the working men in Greenock live. All the more trustworthy that it is drawn by themselves. . . All that has been said relates to physical health. What is to be said as to moral health, when the overcrowded dwellings do not admit of even a separation between the sexes?" The corrected death-rate was 39·0 in 1863, and 38·0 in 1864, as stated by Dr. Buchanan,* to whose admirable "Report on Epidemic Typhus at

---

* "Eighth Report of the Medical Officer of the Privy Council." Appendix pp. 209-225.

Greenock" I refer those who desire further information, as to the condition of this populous and thriving seaport of the West of Scotland.

If we multiply by the hundred these two dark but faithful pictures, we shall have some faint idea of the extent to which overcrowding and its accompaniments of indecency, immorality, and disease prevail throughout the kingdom, many rural districts rivalling in unwholesomeness, both physical and moral, the worst parts of our crowded cities, regarding which Mr. Hole makes the following just remarks : * "The statements are not true of one, or of a few large towns, but of all. Whenever the sanitary state of any place comes to be investigated, the same revelations appear. Whether in the large towns of England, Scotland, or Ireland—such as Liverpool, Birmingham, Leeds, Glasgow, Edinburgh, or Dublin—there is the same complaint of overcrowding among large portions of the population, the same mingling of the sexes in one common room, where sleeping, cooking, eating, washing, have all to be performed, the same shutting up of the population in courts and back streets, and the same recklessness of human health and of all that ennobles life and makes it worth having." And the evil, far from being stationary, is yearly increasing. " I could tell you much," writes Mr. Davies from Bristol, " concerning the evils of overcrowding on the morals of the poor, and the re-action of this on the classes above ; on the unchastity and incest which arise from it ; on the established fact that sound morals have their physical conditions as well as sound bodily health ; on the alarming extent of infanticide ; on the increase of prostitution ; on the growing materialism and separation of classes in large towns ; on the evils arising from new modes of trade, &c., &c. By so doing, I should tire both you and myself, for the subject is anything but an inviting one." In Carlisle, the accommodation is " very varied— some very bad, but not nearly so much so as in many of the larger towns." In Chester, " the lodgings are chiefly small and in closely confined districts ; they are under the Lodging House Act of 1851 ; there has been no attempt to start model lodging-houses. The inspector is now re-adjusting the numbers allowed by the Act, so as to reduce their overcrowded state. He proposes to have a minimum allowance of 300 cubic feet for each adult." In Doncaster, "houses are scarce and dear, and lodging accommodation bad and deficient." In Dundee, " very deficient, as in all manufacturing towns." In King's Lynn, "there is an abundance of small tenements at very moderate rents, but as a rule they are too crowded, and ill-ventilated, and not well cared for in the matter of privies." In Leeds, where, as we have seen, the system of back to back houses, and the want of privy accommodation have long been among the leading nuisances complained of, " the question of overcrowding is one difficult to deal

* " Homes of the Working Classes," p. 22. See also " The Danger of Deterioration of Race," &c., by John Edward Morgan, M.A., M.D., Oxon ; Soc. Sc. Transactions, 1865, p. 427. Also in pamphlet form. Longmans, 1866.

with until house accommodation is provided on a more extensive scale than at present. There are a few model lodging-houses of which the working classes avail themselves." In Liverpool, " the lodging-houses, like the ordinary dwellings of the working-classes are, as a rule, very badly constructed. There are only four model lodgings in the town, and these are only capable of accommodating 429 lodgers. The number of registered lodging-houses of all descriptions amounts to 1,250. There are one chief and four sub-inspectors of lodging-houses. Besides the inspectors of lodging-houses, there are four inspectors to discover cases of overcrowding in houses not registered as lodging-houses ; they are called inspectors of sub-let houses. During the last year the convictions were, for—

" Overcrowding	25
" Mixing Sexes	14
" Not Registering	27
" Not Exhibiting Tickets	7
" Not Applying for Tickets.	4
" Not Washing Floors	12
" Not Sweeping Floors	28
" Not Lime-washing Rooms	7
	" 124."

In Maidstone, " during the hop-picking, immense numbers of the lowest population from London resort here and to the district in general, and are packed closely together. At times they suffer fearfully from cholera and other diseases. They are better looked after than they formerly were, and no time is lost in remitting them to their homes when their work is done." In Merthyr Tydfil, " as a rule, overcrowding takes place among the Irish ; otherwise rare among the Welsh. Number of lodgers in Welsh cottages two, *i.e.* one bed." Newcastle, as fully detailed in Dr. Julian Hunter's report,* "contains a sample of the finest tribe of our countrymen, often sunk by external circumstances of house and street into an almost savage degradation." The lodging accommodation is very deficient, and in certain localities, especially near large manufactories, they are at a premium, and sub-letting is resorted to in order to re-duce excessive rents. Newport (Monmouth) is "very much over-crowded ; the accommodation for the existing population is quite inadequate. Eighteen prosecutions were instituted last year for overcrowding, owing to which we suffered," writes Dr. Davies, "from an epidemic, or rather endemic of typhus, which caused 110 deaths ; and if Christison's estimate of the mortality from typhus (viz. 1 in 10) be correct, it must have attacked 1,100 people. The 35th section of the Sanitary Act, 1866, has just been adopted in the town at my advice ; but much good cannot be done till more houses are

---

* Eighth Report of Medical Officer of Privy Council, pp. 50, 145, 157.

built for the working classes. To work this section on anything like a large scale would necessitate turning out half our population into the streets. All, therefore, that can now be done is to select some of the worst fever nests, and endeavour to diminish the overcrowding of them. Owing to the difficulty of obtaining land for building, and the high ground-rents demanded, there seems to be no inducement for speculators to build more workmens' houses, which is our greatest want at present." In Northampton there is "a great deal of overcrowding, and in villages, three beds frequently in a room." In Norwich, " the working classes live principally in small cottages, or old tenements, and in rooms; many of the latter are let ready-furnished. A large number of these dwelling-places are *Corporation property, and are of a very inferior description.* The new dwellings recently built and in course of erection on the outskirts of the town are much better. There are only six registered common lodging-houses in Norwich, but there are 613 public-houses (besides beer-houses), nearly all of which receive lodgers, on account of the small number of the registered houses." In Portsmouth, " lodging accommodation for the working classes is very bad; in some other parts of the borough fairly good; but vast numbers of small houses have been built in all parts without any due regard to the making and lighting of streets, paving, or drainage ; and many parts of the borough are in a disgraceful condition." In Sheffield, most of the artizans "have a house of their own, and those who live in the suburbs have frequently a garden. The average number of inmates to each house is rather more than five, and many of these dwellings either front the street, or open into moderately-sized yards. There is probably less of the confined alley and narrow *cul-de-sac* in Sheffield than in many manufacturing towns. A good deal has been done of late years to the sewers and surface drains of the town, but still much requires to be done to improve the sanitary condition of the inhabitants. The working classes appear but little aware that they have a duty to perform as well as the authorities," and " do what the authorities may, their efforts will be far from successful, if a nidus of morbific effluvia be permitted to remain in almost every part of the confined courts in which the houses of some of our artizans are placed, and who, on opening their windows with the forlorn hope of purifying their small habitations with the breezes of summer, get instead a mixture of gases from dunghills, ashpits, and night-soil—or what is even worse, because more insidious, from earth which has become impregnated with organic matter imbibed long before, and which now, though comparatively clean and dry, emits a poisonous vapour." * In South Shields "accommodation is difficult to get, old houses and alleys are consequently overcrowded ; proceedings rarely taken, though much needed." In the old part of Sunderland accommodation is very limited—" back to back in

---

* "The Effects of Sheffield Trades on Life and Health," &c., by John Charles Hall, M.D., *Soc. Sc. Transactions,* 1865, p. 384. Also in pamphlet form. Longmans, 1865. 2nd edition, p. 5.

hundreds of instances," says Dr. Julian Hunter, "so arranged that no out-door place could be found where even the public could build privies." In the remaining part of the borough, however, the dwellings are very good. Proceedings have been taken against several parties for overcrowding during the two years preceding Midsummer, 1866.

Mr. Hole gives a most interesting account of what has been and is being done to remedy this alarming defect in our social economy. But while he does justice to the efforts of my old and much valued friends, Mr. Henry Roberts and the Rev. Dr. Begg, I miss from among the names of those he has mentioned as the pioneers of this great national enterprise, the late Rev. Dr. Gilly, of Norham, who nearly thirty years ago, if I mistake not, first drew public attention to the evils of the "bothy" system in the northern counties of England ; and the Rev. Charles (now Canon) Girdlestone, whose "Letters on the Unhealthy Condition of the Lower Class of Dwellings, especially in Large Towns," published in 1845, did much to make known the results of the inquiries of the Health of Towns Commission, and to awaken an interest in the efforts then beginning to be made for the improvement of the condition of the labouring classes. I am happy to see, from his recent denunciations (in the *Times*) of the scandalous state of the cottages of agricultural labourers in various parts of the country, that long familiarity with this gigantic evil has not lessened his abhorrence of the physical and moral degradation that directly flows from it, or the zeal that prompts his earnest and persevering efforts for its removal. The following extracts from the returns and other documents that have been furnished to me, will be both interesting and encouraging.

In Aberdeen, "several gentlemen have taken up the subject of houses for the working classes; and there is one company at least now making up as quickly as they can for the several hundred miserable old houses knocked down for railway purposes." In Birkenhead, where "the proceedings hitherto taken under the Nuisances Removal Act, have mostly been satisfactory, there is plenty of good cottage accommodation to be had at present, and all new cottages are erected under regulations similar to those of the model bye-laws. They are regularly inspected by the inspector of nuisances, and are all in excellent order." In Bradford, where the building bye-laws are admirably fitted to secure well-constructed and well-aired dwellings for the labouring population, "the authorities are not able to enforce the law against overcrowding for want of sufficient houses. But two large blocks of houses are in course of erection by means of subscription, but intended to be self-paying. These buildings are designed as models. Accommodation of this kind has been very deficient, and it is hoped that the experiments now being made will lead to more extended efforts." In Gateshead, "the older portions of the town are very bad, the houses generally being ill-constructed, ill-ventilated, and, as a rule, overcrowded. A very large number of houses consisting of two storeys, designed for two families, have recently been built, and the erection of others is going on with incredible rapidity; but the demand for these houses far exceeds the supply. The houses consist of two rooms on the ground floor and three on the upper, each tenant having a separate entrance, and one ample yard common to both. The yards are paved and well drained. Some have waterclosets; generally, however, ash-pits and privies. The streets are not less than 40 feet wide. There are seven common lodging-houses in Gateshead, licensed for 206 persons. These are regularly inspected, and the Act strictly enforced. They are exceedingly clean and well kept, and may serve as models to the tenement houses in their vicinity. It is exceedingly rare to meet with a case of infectious disease in them; and during my tenure of office, I have not met with a single case of fever in one of them. Four of them are in Pipewellgate, and although, in my opinion, not what lodging houses should be, yet the rigid enforcement of sanitary measures suffices to prevent infectious disorders, although in the surrounding tenement houses zymotic disease is rarely if ever absent, nor ever will be, until the same law is applied to tenement property as to lodging-houses."

We have already seen what sweeping changes are contemplated by the Glasgow Town Council under their new Police and Improvement Act. Dr. Littlejohn* gives two striking "specimens of what will become of your courts and closes, should proprietors be allowed to run up skeleton houses of the most ricketty description and faulty sanitary construction. Both are inhabited by the very poor; but Birtley Buildings is a refuge for some of the worst characters in the town. Each room is small and overcrowded, the passages are dark and ill-ventilated. On all sides you have vice in its most repulsive forms. With an Inspector of Buildings, armed with sufficient powers, such monstrosities in dwellings for the poor would never have been permitted. Tried by any standard, they are faulty in the extreme. A similar plea cannot be urged in their behalf as may be put forth for older houses in the city—that at first they were inhabited by a better class and were not overcrowded, but have sunk gradually into their present condition. Birtley Buildings and Crombie's Land, on the other hand, are modern structures, built specially for the poor, and with an eye to a large rental; hence the small ill-ventilated rooms, and their great deficiency in sanitary comforts." Such were the worthless dwellings built by unprincipled and short-sighted speculators for the "well-to-do industrious workman," who left them to the occupancy of the dregs of society as soon as substantial comfortable quarters were provided elsewhere. Such are the houses of which 16 have been built in various parts of Edinburgh between 1851 and 1864. Some of these I have inspected with great pleasure; but what interested me even more deeply was the thoroughly successful experiment of Dr. Robert Foulis, who showed how much may be accomplished by a single individual and at a moderate outlay, in providing accommodation for the poorer classes,

* Report on the Sanitary Condition of Edinburgh, p. 33.

who cannot afford to pay the average yearly rent of £6 or £7 charged in the model buildings. "He took a close in the Grass Market,* gutted it, cleaned it thoroughly, and repaired it, in on expensive manner, but in such a way as to afford comfortable housing for the poor. This close, the Warden's Close, No. 139, has thus been reclaimed. It is placed under such supervision, that the inhabitants are taught cleanliness, and should a new comer not be susceptible of the lesson, after a patient trial, he quickly leaves. To this hour the close in question stands out an oasis amidst the wretchedness and filth that is to be met with in other closes of that well-known locality. Had this example been followed by our philanthropic citizens who have subscribed so handsomely to the various building schemes, some of the worst localities in the Old Town might have been renovated, crime and pauperism rooted out from them, and the workmen comfortably housed in situations possessing a good exposure and a healthy site. A more admirable situation for such buildings than the district of the Canongate, can hardly be seen anywhere, whether altitude, exposure, or drainage facilities be taken into account." How much has been done in London in the way both of improving old, and of building new houses, by the various societies which have been established during the last 25 years,—foremost among them the Metropolitan Association for Improving the Dwellings of the Industrial Classes, and the Association for Improving the Condition of the Labouring Classes—is well known to many not only in London but throughout the kingdom. Equally well known and appreciated are the achievements of Mr. Alderman Waterlow and the Peabody Trustees, in the Metropolis ; of Mr. Titus Salt, at Saltaire ; of Mr. Akroyd and the Crossleys at Halifax ; and of the Freehold Land Society, under the direction of Mr. James Taylor, at Birmingham. So gratifying has been the success of Mr. Crossley's efforts during the past 15 years, that he has recently erected another lodging house, and Mr. Hole announces† that, "acting upon the example set by Mr. Akroyd, nine gentlemen constituted themselves a ' Society for the Erection of Improved Dwellings.' As opportunity has offered, they have purchased small plots of land in different parts of Leeds, and erected houses thereon, at prices ranging from £150 to £200 per house, including land and all expenses. By building a lot together, the land, materials, legal charges, architect's commission, and other expenses, were reduced much below what they would have cost if erected by an individual. A working man is thus able to obtain a cottage at cost price. He is expected to provide one-fifth of the purchase money, and the remaining four-fifths is advanced to him by the building society at 4½ per cent. The building society is repaid (both principal and interest) by a contribution equal in amount to what he would ordinarily have to pay in rent for a similar house, spread over a period of thirteen years and a half." ‡

---

* Dr. Littlejohn's Report, p. 40. † Page 87.

‡ On this subject see "The Prevention of Pauperism, and Suggestions for a Mode of Supplying Cheap and Healthy Dwellings, &c.," by Dr. Hawksley.

In Newcastle-upon-Tyne, a sub-committee was lately appointed by the Public Health Committee, " to inquire into the number of houses in the borough let as tenements; their water supply, ventilation, ashpit and privy accommodation, and drainage ; the number of their occupants, and the cubic space allowed for each ; to ascertain to what extent, amongst what class, and under what conditions, zymotic diseases have been most fatal during the past twelve months ; to consider the cost of such diseases to the community ; and report on all these matters, and generally upon the sanitary state of the borough, and the means of improving it, but especially upon the advisability and practicability, under the direction of the corporation, of opening up new streets in crowded districts; for sweeping away old dilapidated and unhealthy dwellings, and of erecting in their stead better and healthier houses and lodging-houses for the labouring classes ; the committee to meet daily until the inquiry is complete."* In Plymouth, " some few cottages have been built for the working classes, in the north-eastern part of the town, as a private speculation ;" and in Reading, Mr. Walford informs me that the accommodation is " good, and that there is a model lodging-house where the charge is threepence a night." In Worcester, as stated by Sir Charles Hastings,* a company, which was formed to purchase the whole of the worst part of the town, raised a sum of £10,000, effected the purchase, and after having cleared away all the old houses, built houses on the old sites on an improved plan. The change for the better in that part of the town was most remarkable, " though it had not answered in a pecuniary point of view. In place of the miserable, vicious, and degraded population which used to inhabit that locality, they had there a population useful as artizans, setting a good example to the poor, and a credit to the city."

From what has been stated in the foregoing pages, it is clear that, while the proportions of *this* social evil are enormous, the energies of the nation are gradually being directed to its removal, and that the adoption by the legislature of judicious measures of encouragement would tend greatly to stimulate the efforts of local reformers. Any enactment likely to prove beneficial must provide for the granting of government loans on easy terms; must facilitate the acquisition, with a good title, of such low house property as the owners shall decline to improve; and must likewise provide for strict government inspection of all new works undertaken and executed by local authorities or associations. I therefore cordially concur in the following suggestions of Dr. Acland : " I think a government inspector ought always to inspect the execution of works when the government sanctions the borrowing of money; and the inspector should publish his reports and certificates. The

---

* This sub-committee, appointed in October, has, I believe, presented its Report, which is now (May, 1867) under consideration.

† *Soc. Sc. Transactions* 1860, page 722 ; and 1864, p. 58.

inspection should be real, and be made during the execution, and before instalments are sanctioned, just as an architect certifies to work done. This will hinder bad work. There is no work which requires more careful execution than drainage works. Improvements in details have been made by Clark, of Carlisle, and others, of which many local contractors and surveyors might be entirely ignorant, but which inspectors with large experience might know and require."

My returns in regard to slaughter-houses are very imperfect, owing to my not having made inquiry regarding them in many of my earlier schedules of queries. But I find that in Aberdare, Birkenhead, Cardiff, Dundee, Edinburgh, Greenock, Newport, Paisley, and Reading, the arrangements are either on the whole or quite satisfactory. In Birkenhead, Edinburgh, Greenock, Newport, and Paisley, as also, I believe in Cardiff, no private slaughter-houses are allowed ; and in Aberdare, Dundee, Paisley, and Reading, where they are permitted, notwithstanding the existence of admirably conducted public abattoirs, they are under special regulations, the infringement of which exposes them to heavy penalties. In Newcastle, where " they are all within the town, slaughter-houses have been erected by the corporation since the cattle disease regulations have been in force, adjacent to the cattle market; charge 1s. for each beast slaughtered. The cattle market is seven acres in extent. There is still a large number of slaughter-houses in various parts of the town, in courts and yards, surrounded by dwelling houses." * In Aberdeen, Gateshead, Leeds, Doncaster, and South Shields, the erection of public abattoirs out of town has been, as in London, talked of for some time, and will, it is hoped, soon be carried out, for in some of those towns, as also in Bristol, many of the private slaughter-houses, though licensed, are very offensive. Is it a subject of congratulation, or the reverse, that we are beginning—only beginning—to act in this matter, on the principles so clearly propounded by Sir John Pringle more than a hundred years ago ?

We now come to consider the drainage and water supply of these towns :—

TOWN.	DRAINAGE.	WATER SUPPLY.
Aberdeen . .	"Good in the principal streets ; either indifferent or altogether wanting in the second-rate and worst streets. A thorough and efficient drainage is being carried out under a recent Act."	Admirable and very abundant. 6,000,000 gallons of the purest water brought into town daily, from a distance of 21 miles, by the New Water Works, in the hands of the Corporation.

* The arrangements in Chichester, as in Stafford, seem to be of a very primitive kind ; a cattle and pig market being held fortnightly in the streets ; and between 200 and 300 pigs being kept in the city.

Town.	Drainage.	Water Supply.
Aberdare . .	——	" Plenty, and of the best quality; in the hands of the Water Works Company."
Birkenhead .	" On the whole, good."	" Generally abundant and good; supplied from works the property of the town, pumped from wells in the new red sandstone."
Birmingham .	" A very elaborate system of deep drainage, not yet quite completed."	" Very variable to poorer districts."
Bradford . .	" A general system of drainage has been laid down under the Public Health Act, plans having been submitted and approved by the Government officer. The work is being proceeded with as rapidly as possible, the worst parts of the town having precedence."	" Complete throughout the town as far as service by the Corporation is concerned; and officers are making house to house inspection in the poorer districts to see that every house is supplied. Presentment was made to the committee of above 100 houses (recently), which had not taken the supply. Supply enforced under the Public Health Act of 1848, as amended by Local Government Act of 1858."
Brighton . .	" Very deficient. Of 42 miles of streets and thoroughfares, only about 13 have intercepting drains; but a complete system of drainage is now commenced, the cost of which will be, when complete, £200,000."	" Excellent and abundant, from springs a mile from town, dip being from the well to the town, so that no contamination can take place."
Bristol . . .	" Over 100 miles of drains, emptying into a tidal river. 50 miles of those drains made during last ten years, all well ventilated."	" Abundance of excellent water supplied by a private company from the Mendip Hills. Some courts are still short of water, or supplied by pumps of a suspicious character. This subject is now under the consideration of our committee, and some notices have been served on landlords."
Cambridge	" Actual drainage of town good, but principle bad. All into the Cam."	" Abundant and pure; water courses in streets, keeping both them and sewers clean."

TOWN.	DRAINAGE.	WATER SUPPLY.
Canterbury.	"Just now in a transition state. We hope it may be well done eventually."	"For the poor mainly by taps situated at various parts of the town. For these, however, we are indebted to our forefathers, *i.e.* it is a very old provision."
Cardiff	"Now very efficient; commenced in 1855, first system completed in 1856."	"First obtained from river Ely ; latterly an additional supply has been obtained from springs connected with the north range of hills, about five miles from Cardiff. Supply to small houses, at 2d. per week, abundant."
Carlisle	"Very good."	"Insufficient and unclean. Obtained from river Eden, which river receives the drainage of several considerable towns above Carlisle; of Penrith, with a population of 7,000 to 8,000 ; Brampton, 2,000 to 3,000 ; Appleby and several others."
Cheltenham	"Very good. Above 25 miles of public sewerage in hands of Commissioners, intercepting ; but much still in private hands. (See Dr. Wilson's Sanitary statistics of Cheltenham, pp, 8-11.)"	"In a transition state—supplied by water company chiefly from the Chelt; other sources of supply under consideration. Severn rejected, owing to its impurity, containing 28 grains of solid matter in the gallon, 4 of which were organic. Supply to poorer districts, bad."
Chichester	"Cesspools in a porous, gravelly soil, and surface drainage. Corporation will not undertake deep drainage works."	"From wells sunk in the gravel near cesspools, which pollute them, so that in numerous instances the water is turbid and filthy, yet the people in many cases drink it as long as they can, and then perhaps apply to a neighbour for some that does not smell or taste so bad. It abounds in animalculæ."
Derby	———	"Constant and plenty of it, but there is a good deal of pump water used in the old houses."

TOWN.	DRAINAGE.	WATER SUPPLY.
Devonport . .	" Extremely imperfect in many parts of the town; in some absolutely none, except by surface gutters."	" Very good. 24 miles of running stream brings it to the reservoir. It contains a grain and a-half of potash in the gallon; generally paid for by landlords. Kept in tanks or water-butts. Several families depend on one supply."
Doncaster . .	" Good, but bad place for out-fall; not into the Dun, but into the 'River Dun Navi-gation,' and so to the Trent."	" 20 pumps in streets; supply good, but hard water; rest obtained from river Dun, which receives the sewage of Sheffield, Rotherham, Masborough, and other towns, containing in all about 300,000 inhabitants."
Dundee . . .	" Perfect."	" The defect in the poorer dis-tricts is that the water is not brought into their houses, although wells are conti-guous to them. The better class of workers have water in their houses."
Edinburgh . .	" Where completed, excellent. House-drainage in many poor districts very imper-fect; in some, impossible. (*See* Report, p. 76-90.) Un-trapped gully-holes, and water of Leith, often very offensive."	" No wells allowed to be used. Supply by water company, who are bound by General Police and Improvement Act to introduce water into all houses. In 1863, 31·12 gal-lons daily for each inhabi-tant. When the new springs have been added to present resources, the daily supply will be 39 gallons per head."
Exeter . . .	" Every part is completely sewered, but there are legal difficulties in compelling a communication with pri-vate houses."	No return. Good, I believe, since 1832, since which water has been uncontami-nated by sewage. .
Gateshead	" Until the last 18 months, very little more than one-third of the borough was properly drained; latterly, however, drainage works have been pursued with great vigour; expected to be complete or nearly so in a year."	" By Newcastle and Gates-head Water Company; bad and dear, besides very pre-carious, as Gateshead has no reservoirs independent of those on the Newcastle side of the river; any accident to the pipes crossing the Tyne would deprive Gateshead of its supply. In the poorer

TOWN.	DRAINAGE.	WATER SUPPLY.
Gateshead . . (*Continued.*)	———	parts of the town, where, from want of yard space, it it has been necessary to erect waterclosets, the want of pressure and the dearness are very great evils, and have rendered sanitary progress much more difficult than it would have been."
Glasgow . .	"Generally very good, but into the river, the state of which is very bad."	Admirable, from Loch Katrine; the model of the whole kingdom. Supply constant. Distribution improving yearly.
Gloucester . .	" Good ; three-fourths of the city drained."	" Not continuous. One ordinary tap supply to each court in poorer districts."
Greenock . .	" Good main drains in nearly every street. In some streets, the proprietors of tenements have not yet communicated with the common sewers."	" The supply for the poorer districts is by public wells, and confessedly very deficient."
Grimsby . .	" Of a temporary character only."	" By Water Works Company. The Local Board of Health have not adopted compulsory powers of supplying the poorer districts, which is much needed, as the wells there are seriously affected by the sewage. The Local Board have issued notices for persons to give information and lodge complaints."
Halifax . .	" Good."	" Abundant in poorer districts."
Hastings . .	" Good and effective, at least in the Health of Towns district, having cost nearly £20,000 a few years ago, but the outlets interfere with the bathing, and occasionally smell badly. To remedy this, the Board have determined to remove the outlets a long distance from the town. The contract is signed for £26,000, and the work is commenced. The	" The poorer districts are well supplied with water."

TOWN.	DRAINAGE.	WATER SUPPLY.
Hastings . . (*Continued.*)	Commissioners of St. Leonard's, are also on the eve of doing the same on the West side for £6,000, The deodorization of the fluid part of the sewage, and conversion of the solid into guano, is about to be tried on a large scale—by heat. Bone dust is added, to supply the deficiency of phosphates."	
Hereford . .	" Good—very good."	" Pretty general, not compulsory, nor unlimited."
Hull . . .	" The east district is well supplied with main drains ; the west also rapidly progressing."	" All the districts of the town are well and amply supplied with good water."
King's Lynn .	——	" Constant and pure to whole town, except in the case of many old houses, which are supplied with water that is allowed to run into underground tanks. This water is often rendered impure, from the close proximity of the privy vaults and cesspools. In some instances the former are placed almost on the top of the water tanks."
Leeds . . .	" Exceedingly deficient in many districts ; but the pollution of streams is very great."	From the Wharfe ; abundant, but much contaminated with the sewage and refuse of various towns.
Leicester . .	" New and good."	" Good and ample for the poor."
Lincoln . .	——	" By water company ; poor supplied at a reduced rate."
Liverpool . .	" 160 miles of sewers, the cost of construction about £281,600."	" Not constant, but is put on twice daily. The average number of hours during which it is on is from six to eight."
Maidstone . .	" Improving, but our rivers are abominably misused and polluted by sewage and refuse from paper mills, gas-works, &c."	" Better than it was, but to the poor still very deficient."

TOWN.	DRAINAGE.	WATER SUPPLY.
Merthyr Tydfil	" A system of drainage was commenced in November, 1865, and is now in progress."	Under the Board of Health since November, 1861; unlimited supply, only three degrees of hardness, free from organic impurity, for an annual payment of twenty-pence per head. (Report on Sanitary Condition of Merthyr Tydfil for 1865, pp. 14—18.)
Newcastle . .	" 14 miles in extent, arterial, into river Tyne; no provision for utilization of sewage."	" Not much to complain of. Reservoirs cover 143 acres, holding 530,000,000 gallons. The corporation pay annually £200 for water, for public grants, urinals, and water closets, and are at present collecting information with a view to proceedings against owners of property who do not provide a proper supply."
Newport . .	" Excellent."	" Constant and plentiful, even in poorer districts."
Northampton.	" No return."	" Not by any means complete in poorer districts, being partly from water .companies, and the remainder from wells, all of which when analysed have been found to contain a great quantity of organic and animal matter; quite unfit for drinking."
Norwich . .	" No return."	" To poorer neighbourhood by pumps and taps; is for the most part very good. The landlord is obliged to lay on water to cottages, if it can be procured at the rate of 2d. per week."
Nottingham .	" Main sewers made by the Highway Committee; private sewers under Sanitary Committee."	" A stand-pipe in each court, with water at high pressure day and night."
Oxford . . .	" Into the rivers. The Cherwell was, till lately, unsullied by drainage. It is now unfit for bathing."	Intermitting; no reservoirs; question of new works referred to Mr. Bateman, C.E.

TOWN.	DRAINAGE.	WATER SUPPLY.
Paisley . . .	Into the river, which is much polluted by it.	" Good, to all inhabitants alike ; from hills to south of town."
Plymouth . .	" For the most part good."	" Intermittent ; for *one* hour daily in some parts of the town, and for *two* hours on alternate days in others."
Portsmouth .	" Generally bad, but a thorough system of drainage is being carried out, at a cost of £100,000."	" For the most part in the hands of a water company, and is adequate to all demands. The poorer tenements are not well supplied, as it is left to the landlords, who charge their tenants about a penny a week per tenement, when they put on the water. The supply is practically uninterrupted."
Reading . .	" At present, cesspools—complete drainage about to be carried out."	" Good and constant, at high pressure."
Sheffield . .	" A good deal has been done of late years to the sewers and surface drains of the town, but still much requires to be done."	By water company, from an elevation of 1,200 feet above the sea level, conveyed in iron pipes into the town, very pure, 4 grains only, to the gallon, of mineral and organic matter. (Dr. J. C. Hall, *Soc. Sc. Transactions* for 1865, p. 385.) Supply to all parts very good.
Shrewsbury .	" Wretched ; into the Severn. About to carry out an extensive system of sewerage, at a cost of £30,000 or £40,000."	" From the Severn for domestic purposes ; drinking water from a spring some distance from town. General water supply to poorer districts very insufficient."
Southampton.	" *Médiocre.* After spending about £20,000 sixteen years ago, it is now contemplated to spend £10,000 more."	" Supply ought to be unlimited (from the Itchen), but is extremely deficient both for poor and rich. Engines too small; others of greater power in course of construction. During the cholera epidemic the poor were shockingly neglected ; they had not enough to cleanse their persons, much less to wash away sewage, &c."

TOWN.	DRAINAGE.	WATER SUPPLY.
South Shields.	" Pretty complete now."	" Very good; from Sunderland and Shields water works."
Stafford . .	"All on the surface, odour at times disgustingly offensive."	" From wells much contaminated by drainage."
Sunderland .	" A most complete system of drainage."	"Ample, and excellent in quality."
Tynemouth .	" The main drainage is very good, but a large number of houses in the oldest part have neither yards nor water-closets."	" Very deficient both for houses and closets, in the oldest part of the town."
Wolverhampton	" The natural drainage good, but main drainage imperfect. A plan has been approved by the Secretary of State, and a thorough system is in contemplation."	" Ample supply to poorer districts is insisted on."
Worcester .	" Perfect."	" Good to poorer districts."

If the foregoing summary is encouraging, as indicating progress in many of the towns enumerated, surely the tardiness of the operations now in hand is fitted to awaken our astonishment. It is very remarkable that in large towns, such as Aberdeen, Birmingham, Brighton, Canterbury, Gateshead, Hull, Leeds, Merthyr Tydfil, Portsmouth, Shrewsbury, and Wolverhampton, the authorities should only now be carrying out, or about to commence, systematic drainage works; and still more so, that in Chichester, Devonport, Grimsby, Reading, and Stafford, the arrangements are wholly, or for the most part, so primitive that the whole soil and the surface wells are becoming continually more impregnated with organic impurities. The pollution of the rivers, again, by the sewage and refuse of Bristol, Cambridge, Chester, Doncaster, Glasgow, Leeds, Maidstone, Manchester, Newcastle, Oxford, Paisley, Sheffield, and Shrewsbury has become a gigantic evil, towards the removal of which the attention and efforts of sanitary reformers should be unceasingly directed.

As regards water supply, while in some places, as in Aberdeen, Cardiff, Glasgow, Merthyr Tydfil, and Sheffield, the arrangements are perfect, and, while in many others they are very satisfactory, it appears that in Birmingham, Cambridge, Canterbury, Dundee, Gateshead, Gloucester, Hereford, Liverpool, Northampton, Norwich,

Nottingham, Oxford, Plymouth, Southampton, and Shrewsbury, there is either no house-supply at all, or that it is sadly deficient, in the poorer districts. In many of these towns, it will be observed, the poor are dependent on pumps or taps, one being often made to serve for a whole court containing a large population—a most defective and objectionable arrangement. But I question whether any part of any town in England will be found in a much worse condition than a district of Kensington, with a return of which I have been favoured by my friend Dr. O'Bryen. It contains 99 houses, with 302 rooms and 970 inhabitants, who are supplied with hard water from three pumps, but receive the company's soft water, when it is on for an hour daily, from leaking butts and cisterns, in pails or pitchers, in which it is kept standing in the close rooms till it is used. No other supply of soft water is available during the remainder of the twenty-four hours, the water in the cisterns being polluted by the gases from the closets above which they are placed. Seventeen houses in one court have each a closet, but with a very insufficient water supply ; while the remaining 82 have 41 closets, a number of them so filthy as to be unfit for use, and only fifteen cisterns and four water butts, containing, after deducting waste, 2,942 gallons—the whole supply, exclusive of pump water, both for domestic purposes and flushing of closets. The entire supply for all purposes to the 99 houses (deducting waste) is 3,611 gallons. The allowance to the 970 inhabitants, at the minimum rate of 15 gallons, should be 14,550 gallons daily. During the prevalence of cholera a few stand pipes were provided, but these have since been removed. It is nearly two years since a committee of the vestry, after very careful examination, gave in their report, recommending the enforcement of stringent measures against the owners, but the vestry, though often urged to act, have as yet done nothing in the way of compelling landlords to provide a sufficient supply of water. The magistrates, when applied to by the vestry to compel landlords to comply with the notices served upon them, have uniformly refused, on the ground that vestries have power, under the Act 25 & 26 Vict. c. 102, to execute the works themselves and recover the costs. Rather than incur the risk, they prefer leaving matters in the disgraceful condition I have described.

In Chichester, Greenock, Grimsby, Northampton, and Stafford, the pump-water, which is consumed by the greater part of the inhabitants, is much contaminated with organic impurities. In Carlisle, Chester, Doncaster, and Leeds, the whole supply is drawn from rivers which receive the sewage of large populations. The case of Doncaster merits special notice. " Our only supply of water," writes Mr. Fairbank, " is from the river Dun ; 18, 12, and 11 miles respectively up this river, stand Sheffield, Rotherham, and Masborough, besides many populous villages. Into this river these places all send their sewage, so that our water is well fecalized before we get it. In July, I heard Dr. Letheby swear on the Four Gospels, before the Lords' Committee, that the sewage of Sheffield (a town containing 216,000 souls) was so far oxidized before it got to Doncaster, that it could do no harm here ; so we go on drinking it, and some people rather like it." If so, the tidings communicated to me by Dr. Hall, that the Sheffield authorities think of keeping the sewage out of the rivers, will not be altogether welcome to some of the inhabitants of Doncaster. *De gustibus non disputandum.* But this doctrine of the speedy conversion, by oxidation, of the sewage and refuse of 300,000 human beings, and of multitudes of animals, clean and unclean, into perfectly innocuous material, has a very suspicious look, especially when placed alongside of Professor Frankland's statement, * that even boiling does not destroy the noxious properties of cholera discharges, when these are diffused in water. The oxidation theory may be true, to the extent alleged by Dr. Letheby, but its probable *laissez faire* results are not pleasant food for thought, nor, I apprehend, for wholesome fish.

With a few striking facts in reference to the propagation of infectious disorders, I conclude this too lengthened paper. In no department of our social economy has the liberty of the subject held more uncontrolled sway than in this death-haunted region of epidemic and infectious disorders. From "my lords" of her Majesty's Privy Council, as we have seen, down to the snuggest parish vestry in the land, there seems to be a prevailing disposition, like Izaak Walton with his worm, to "handle them tenderly as though we loved them." The means for limiting their ravages are in our hands ; the discovery of the agent that gives effectual protection against the most deadly and loathsome of them all is one of the hygienic glories of England; yet the United Kingdom is the chosen *habitat* of typhus, and the mortality from small-pox is greater in the country of Jenner than in any other country of Europe. We know that the prompt isolation of persons smitten with infectious diseases, and the emptying and cleansing and lime-washing of those dwellings which furnish a steady—often a perennial—supply of such cases, will assuredly prevent their multiplication ; yet though in almost every town from which I have received returns, cholera hospitals were being provided, and " disinfectants," such as quicklime, chlorides of lime and zinc, carbolic acid, sulphate of iron, and McDougall's powder, were being liberally used, in only a very few have any systematic efforts been made to limit the prevalence of communicable disease. We have already seen how thoroughly and speedily successful were the measures taken in 1865 to arrest the spread of typhus in Bristol ; and in Birkenhead, the energetic proceedings of Dr. Robinson were followed in the same year by a remarkable diminution in the mortality from contagious diseases. In his first report (for 1864), speaking of scarlatina, he says, " means should therefore be devised to check the progress of this epidemic by early isolation of the sufferers; and before the convalescent is again permitted to enter into the society of

---

* *Times*, Sept. 5, 1866.

the healthy, copious ablutions, together with the use of disinfectants, should be resorted to; and those clothes which cannot be purified by washing, &c., should be exposed to a dry heat of 206°. Fahr. The interesting experiments of Dr. Henry and others have clearly shown the value of dry heat as a destroyer of the specific poisons which produce contagious diseases.* The Health Committee of Liverpool, acting under the advice of their intelligent medical officer of health, are taking the initiative steps towards providing a public building for the purpose of washing, disinfecting, and exposing to dry heat the clothes of those who have suffered from contagious diseases, and I trust that, attached to the fever wards about to be built in connection with the Birkenhead union, a similar provision will be made." This suggestion has been acted on. In his report for 1865, he gives the following summary of sanitary operations during the year :—" Pigs were removed from 62 places where the keeping of them was a cause of nuisance to the neighbourhood; 124 privies have been converted into water-closets; 21 pits of stagnant water were drained; 2,451 nuisances arising from obstruction of drains, defective traps, &c., were reported by the inspector, and proceedings taken to remedy the same; 4,827 houses, containing 19,263 apartments, were visited with a view to improving their sanitary condition; 1,043 lime-washing notices were served upon the occupiers of dirty houses, and attended to by them; 25 cellars, used as dwellings, were vacated; 70 overcrowded houses had their numbers reduced; 37 persons were convicted before the magistrates of offences against sanitary laws, and penalties amounting in the aggregate to £18 10s. inflicted." That the sudden fall exhibited in the following table is in some degree owing to these precautions, it is only reasonable to infer.

DEATHS FROM	1864.	1865.
Small Pox	121	37
Scarlatina	81	37
Measles	76	21
Typhus (including Typhoid Fever)...	71	63
	349	158

The other towns which have either fever hospitals or fever wards for the isolation of the patients are Carlisle, Derby, Edinburgh, Gates-head, Glasgow, Greenock, Hull, Leicester, Maidstone (at union

* See an excellent paper "On the Disinfecting Property of Heat," in the *Soc. Sc. Transactions* for 1864, by Dr. Shann of York, pp. 556-563.

infirmary three miles from town), Manchester, Newcastle, and, I believe, Sunderland. Liverpool, besides fever wards attached to the Workhouse Infirmary, has another fever hospital available for other classes. In Glasgow, where the enforcement of strict police regulations in common lodging-houses, and the early removal of patients to one or other of the hospitals, have made a decided impression on the endemic typhus, there are not less than five fever hospitals—one at the Royal Infirmary, the City of Glasgow Fever Hospital under the magistrates and town council, and three others under the parochial boards. " There is also a regular service of disinfection and a special washing-house for the clothes of infected persons. This is done without charge, on the order of the medical officer." In Liverpool " a disinfecting apparatus on Henry's principle was erected in the north district, and ready for use in February 1866 ; another is ordered for the south-end of the town." In his report for 1858, Mr. Moore states that he was led, in consequence " of the rapid extension of scarlet fever, measles, &c., in their respective neighbourhoods, whenever these diseases appeared in them," to institute special inquiries into the state of the 'Dames' schools, in Leicester. It turned out that in eleven of them the cubic space for each child varied from $26\frac{1}{2}$ to $58\frac{3}{4}$, though in only two did it exceed 42 cubic feet. In two, each had only $26\frac{1}{2}$, and in two others $28\frac{1}{2}$ cubic feet, an allowance suggestive of suffocation to the tiny pupils. Since then the dames' schools have been frequently visited, and placed under regulations which are strictly enforced, very much to the advantage of the health not only of the children but of the town. In 1864, when 104 persons died of small-pox, he vainly repeated a recommendation he had previously made, that an institution should be provided for the reception of small-pox cases, which are excluded from the fever-house, and must be treated at their lodgings, with the certain result of an extension of the disease to others in the house and surrounding neighbourhood. In Edinburgh, there is, in the bye-laws for common lodging-houses, a special provision " that in case of fever, cholera, or other contagious, infectious, or epidemic disease occurring in such lodging-house, whether to any lodger or to any other person residing or being in such house, the keeper of such house who shall neglect or omit forthwith to give notice thereof to the superintendent of police, in order that the nature of the complaint may be ascertained, shall, for every such neglect and omission, be liable in a penalty not exceeding forty shillings." The result is seen in the following statement (p. 36 of Dr. Littlejohn's report) : "It is certainly remarkable that, of the 163 cases of death from fever (in 1863) not one occurred in these the poorest and most crowded houses in Edinburgh. . . . Of course the overcrowded state of their population renders them the hotbeds of disease in epidemic years, and when cholera and fever were raging, these houses attained an unenviable notoriety. Were not unusual facilities presented in Edinburgh—the seat of a medical school—for the speedy treatment of the sick, and the removal of cases of infectious disease to our noble charity, the Royal

Infirmary, a single case of fever allowed to run its course unwatched in such tenements would spread contagion all sides, and the district mortality would be greatly increased." Such, however, is the case in most towns throughout the kingdom. The general reply to my inquiry as to the isolation and conveyance of persons ill of infectious disorders is, " no attention is paid to the isolation of such patients."

"There is another mode* of mediate communication, the mere mention of which excites astonishment at the apathy that permits the continuance of a practice by which a large amount of preventible disease is occasioned. I allude to the common practice of conveying patients, known to be labouring under or convalescing from highly contagious disorders, in hackney carriages. That this is the mode of infection in cases which every now and then startle the fashionable world, e. g. the death by small-pox of a distinguished Italian diplomatist about two years ago (1860), is in the highest degree probable. At a small reunion of medical men the summer before last (1861) in the house of my friend Dr. Cotton, one of the company detailed the following instructive case which had fallen under his notice some weeks before. It was suggested by the mention of the sudden death, from small-pox, of Mr. Henry Gray, of St. George's Hospital. The gentleman in question hailed a cab, and told the cabman to drive to a certain number in a fashionable west-end street. He went in to see his patient, but found his services no longer required. She had died of small-pox. When he came out, the cabman, who had been struck by the closed window-shutters, asked if there was any one ill within? My friend replied in the affirmative, and ordered him to drive to another address. He had given him his fare, and was about to leave, when the man, to his surprise, asked if any one had died in the last house they had been at? An affirmative reply elicited the involuntary exclamation, " Oh ! Lord," and the explanation that, on a certain day, having just put down a small-pox patient, he was hailed by a lady, whom he had conveyed to the house where she now lay dead." Was this, I ask, a case of "justifiable homicide?" In my opinion it should be made a felony. A society has been formed in London for the provision of ambulances for infectious cases, and has already been very successful in its operations; but so far as the vestries and local boards are concerned, the enabling clause of Acts 1860 and 1866 may be said to have been quite inoperative. Here is the result of my inquiries as to the arrangements in other towns :—

Aberdeen. " Three litters at call when wanted."

Birkenhead.—" One special carriage for conveying infectious cases was provided some years ago, but another one was added six months ago on account of the approach of the cholera. I cannot learn any case where a cab-driver has been convicted of conveying

---

* I quote from one of my lectures on medicine, as delivered at the Middlesex Hospital in October, 1862.

infectious cases. When they have been observed doing so, it has been found they have used 'unlicensed cabs,' alleged by them to be used for that purpose only. We have a hackney carriage bye-law, as follows :—'The driver or owner of any such carriage shall not knowingly carry or convey therein any person afflicted with any infectious or contagious disease, or any dead body.' The penalty for so doing is 20s."

Bradford.—" A van is kept at the workhouse for the purpose. Cab owners are prosecuted if they allow their cabs to be used for conveyance of persons ill of infectious disorders."

Bristol.—" The different boards of guardians have each an ambulance for the removal of infectious patients."

Carlisle.—" One at the Fever Hospital."

Chester.—" Fever cases are taken into the infirmary and paid for by the parishes at the rate of 1s. per day. The infirmary provides a sedan chair for the conveyance of the sick. Small-pox is *not* admitted."

Derby.—" No doubt cabs are employed ; but many are brought in a hand-fly, which is to be had on application at the hospital."

Doncaster.—" We hire an old one. Ordinary cabs are not used here, as far as we know, for any one suffering from a contagious disorder. We should not allow it, but proceed under our bye-law against any one so using a public cab."

Dundee.—" Two conveyances specially so used, and for nothing else ; cabs may be used also at times."

Edinburgh.—" A special vehicle is provided. No cabs allowed to be used."

Gateshead.—" The guardians have one carriage for the removal of fever cases."

Glasgow.—" Several vehicles for the conveyance of such cases."

Greenock.—" Fever cases can be conveyed by a special cab, the property of the infirmary. There is also a sedan chair used only for infectious diseases."

Hull.—" We have no separate carriages for the conveyance of fever cases. I think there is a sedan at the workhouse occasionally used."

Leeds.—" There is only one conveyance for the purpose of removing infected persons ; this is supplied by the guardians of the poor."

Leicester.—Liable to a penalty not exceeding 40s. under following bye-law : "No carriage licensed by the local board shall be used for conveying any corpse, or any person who is ill of fever, or of any infectious or contagious disease."

Liverpool.—" Separate carriages—one for typhus, and one for small-pox cases—were provided in November, 1864. They are kept at the public offices, where there is a night watchman, and they are hired by contract. No charge is made for their use. These are quite independent of the fever and small-pox carriages kept by the vestries for the use of paupers. At the commencement of the cholera epidemic, another carriage was provided for cholera patients."

Maidstone.—" One for taking people to the 'union' three miles from town, a stout prejudice existing against the admission even of typhoid fever into the West Kent Hospital."

Manchester.—" The fever hospital has special conveyances at its service."

Newcastle.—" One carriage for the removal of infectious cases is provided by the fever hospital authorities; no other in the town."

Newport.—" No carriages provided by the town, but the guardians of the poor have a species of litter for conveying persons to the workhouse hospital."

Paisley.—" One ambulance is attached to the infirmary for this purpose."

Reading.—" A Bath chair is employed."

Sunderland.—" A carriage is kept solely for the conveyance of persons ill of infectious disorders."

So that some provision is made—and in Birkenhead, Bradford, Bristol, Doncaster, Edinburgh, Glasgow, Leicester, and Liverpool it is very effectual—against the admitted evils that flow from this inexcusable infraction of the laws of health, in 24 of the 59 towns regarding which I have made special inquiries, and also in the metropolis. But in the remaining 35, the liberty of the subject to keep up this dance of death is absolutely unchecked, except in Stafford, where cabs, which are used for the conveyance of all other sick people, are forbidden to take undoubted cases of small-pox. In the name of common sense, of humanity, and, above all, of economy, that god of our idolatry, what hinders that the provision of special means of conveyance for infectious cases should be made compulsory on all local authorities, and that the prohibition, under a penalty, of their conveyance in public carriages, known by experience to work well in those towns where it is in force, should be made universal throughout the kingdom?

In Liverpool alone, so far as I can discover, have any steps been taken towards providing proper receiving-houses for the dead. " Since the passing of the Public Health Act, 1866," writes Dr. Trench, " the council have ordered the erection of two mortuaries. A protestant gentleman, Mr. Hutchinson, is about to erect, at a probable cost of £5,000, a mortuary *Chapel* for the Roman Catholics."

A few words in conclusion on convalescent institutions. It is now nearly fourteen years since I projected, and repeatedly discussed with the late Admiral Percy, then chairman of the Walton Convalescent Institution, a plan for collecting statistics from the London Hospitals, Infirmaries, and Dispensaries, in order to shew the urgent need of a great effort to increase, at least tenfold, the convalescent accommodation for the metropolis. To my great regret I was prevented, by lack of leisure, from carrying out my intentions. Since then some progress has been made. In establishing the institution at Seaford, the Marquis of Townshend and his fellow-workers have conferred a great boon on the sick poor of London; several of the large hospitals are, I believe, providing accommodation in the country for their convalescents; and Mrs. Gladstone is setting an example worthy of all imitation by social reformers throughout the country. My returns on this subject are not complete, as I neglected to put the question to some of my correspondents. But I find, from Dr. Fleming, that Birmingham is now providing itself with an establishment capable of containing 40 inmates; Carlisle has its seaside institution at Silloth; Dundee, Edinburgh, and Glasgow have each a convalescent home, and steps are being taken to provide one for Paisley. In Greenock, "there was, during a late epidemic, a convalescent house for fever patients, but it is now disused." The Newcastle-upon-Tyne Convalescent Society have lately issued their seventh annual report,* which gives a very gratifying account of the increasing usefulness of their convalescent home at Marsden. In Liverpool, there are "no public convalescent institutions; but one has been established by private beneficence in Everton." Mr. Joseph Adshead, in a paper to which I listened with much pleasure at Glasgow in 1860,† announced that he would "shortly submit a plan for a convalescent establishment for Manchester and the surrounding district," but I am informed that his enlightened proposals have not yet been carried into effect. From 23 towns I have received the answer, that nothing has been done in the way of providing such institutions; but Bath, if it has none for itself, is a convalescent establishment on the grand scale for "multitudes of halt, withered, and impotent folk," who repair thither from all parts of England, and often find the healing they had elsewhere sought in vain.

The time, I trust, is not far distant, when a convalescent home will be reckoned an indispensable adjunct to every large town in the kingdom. It would enormously increase the influence for good of our hospitals and dispensaries. The object is so purely beneficent, that it should engage the sympathy and the liberal support of all well-wishers of the sick poor. The wealthy cannot bestow their largesses; the benevolent, whether wealthy or not, their good words and willing gifts; nor the active philanthropist his most earnest efforts, on a truer charity, or one more fruitful of good results. Nor could the guardians of the poor apply a portion of their funds in any way so likely to yield a large remunerative return, not only by improving the public health, but by effecting a permanent reduction of the rates, as in contributing towards the erection or support of convalescent institutions. "Ample funds," to adopt the concluding words of a pamphlet I published in 1849,‡ "would thus be provided for the supply of certain health-giving remedies, of which the medical attendant well knows the value, but for want of which dispensary practice is too often a solemn mockery. Of these I might instance several,

---

* The Eighth, for 1866-67, has just reached me.

† *Soc. Sc. Transactions* for 1860, p.726.

‡ "Sanitary Economics, or our Medical Charities, as they are, and as they ought to be." By A. P. Stewart. M.D.

but I content myself with directing special attention to the facilities that would thereby be afforded, for sending to the country or the coast such patients (and their name is legion) as are pining away for want, not of drugs and elegant prescriptions, but of nature's balmy breath, which never fans the fevered cheeks, or braces the withered frames of the myriads who yearly sink unnoticed from their dark and plague-haunted dwellings into an 'ever yawning and never satisfied grave.'"

The results, then, of eighteen years of sanitary legislation is that we have in the metropolis a large staff of able and active but under-paid officers of health, whose recommendations may be adopted and enforced, or passed by in silence, or rejected with contempt, according to the temper or interests of the different vestries or local boards; that the great majority of the towns throughout the kingdom have no medical officers of health, and that, in those which have them, their remuneration is, with three or four exceptions, shamefully inadequate; and that their position of dependence on the local authorities is such as often to make them comparatively powerless for good, especially when, as sometimes happens, the authorities are interested in the perpetuation of the abuses which their sanitary officers seek to remove. We find also, that the appointment, as is commonly the case, of a single inspector of nuisances, where there ought to be a dozen or more, serves rather to conceal than to bring to light and remove the evils, both physical and moral, so prevalent in our large towns; that both in the metropolis and elsewhere their numbers are, with a few memorable exceptions, so small as to make the discharge of their duties a hopeless task, and that in not a few instances they are burdened with other duties that occupy the most of their time; that, as a rule, the rural districts, which require it nearly as much as the towns, and our ports and harbours * which require it even more, are virtually without any inspection at all; that the great and growing deficiency of lodging accommodation for the labouring-classes necessitates overcrowding, while it prevents the enforcement of the laws enacted for its abatement; and that, owing to the non-appointment of the officers charged with its execution, or the appointment of incompetent ones, the Act for the seizure of diseased and unwholesome articles of food is too commonly a dead letter. We find, moreover, that in many districts the death-rate is increasing, and that, owing to the neglect of vaccination and other sanitary measures, and the very general conveyance of infectious cases in public carriages, the ravages of small-pox and typhus are in many places alarmingly great; that the main and house drainage of many towns is still in a very unsatisfactory state; that the pollution of our streams and rivers is a crying abomination; that the water supply to the poorer districts, both of the metropolis and of other towns, is exceedingly defective; and that, except in a few towns, the work of providing convalescent accommodation for the sick poor has not yet been begun. From all this we conclude that—

---

* *See* an admirable article in the *Times* of Sept. 26, 1866.

1. We require a thoroughly efficient administrative department of government for the superintendence of all matters relating to the public health, and the enforcement of the law on recusant local authorities.

2. The appointment of officers of health, not only in towns, but in the country, and for our ports and harbours, should be compulsory; they should be independent of the local authority, their appointment, the amount of their salary, and their dismissal being subject to the approval of the central department; and should exercise a general supervision of such districts as may be agreed upon.

3. The inspectors of nuisances should always be under the control of the officers of health, and should not be burdened with other and inconsistent duties. Their appointment should in every case be compulsory.

4. There should be an annual return to Parliament of all officers of health and inspectors of nuisances, of the population and areas of their respective districts, of the salaries paid to them, and of the duties they are required to discharge.

5. As a general rule, the officers of health should be specially trained and set apart for that work alone, and be remunerated accordingly, out of the municipal funds or county rates, aided from the consolidated fund.

6. The isolation of those sick of infectious disorders should be enforced by their early removal to—

7. District hospitals or refuges to be provided by the local authorities.

8. The conveyance of such cases in hackney carriages should be everywhere prohibited under a penalty, the same to be strictly enforced against offenders.

9. Carriages for the conveyance of such cases *must* be provided by the local authorities.

10. Disinfecting apparatus for clothes and bedding must likewise be provided by local authorities.

11. We urgently need a well-considered Act, which shall facilitate the acquisition of low house property, and shall empower the government to grant loans on easy terms, on the security of the new buildings, to those who shall undertake to provide wholesome dwellings for the labouring population.

12. The supply of gas and water should be taken out of the hands of private companies, and entrusted to public and responsible bodies, in the interest of the consumer.

13. It should be made lawful for Boards of Guardians to apply a portion of the rates to the providing of convalescent accommodation for those who require, but cannot procure it.

14. A strict government inspection should be made during the progress of all works, for the execution of which the government sanctions the borrowing of money, and before instalments are sanctioned, the inspector's reports and certificates being published.

SANITARY QUERIES.

1. Town?

2. Population { According to last census
   estimated?

3. Medical Officer of Health?

4. Date of appointment?

5. When was office first instituted?

6. Salary, increased, diminished, or stationary?

7. Area of district?

8. Duties required of him?

9. If allowed to practise?

10. Inspectors of Nuisances { Ordinary staff?
    Duties?
    Salaries?
    Extraordinary?

11. Under the control of the officer of health?

12. Inspectors of common lodging-houses?

13. Inspectors of markets and slaughter-houses?

14. What qualifications, if any, required of these various inspectors?

15. If chosen from the police?

16. Discharge of duties efficient?

17. Seizure of unwholesome articles of food, to whom confided? Convictions
    frequent?

18. Drainage { Main, thorough and general?
    House, efficient?
    Intercepting?
    Into rivers, or sea?

19. Water { Whence obtained?
    Quality?
    Supply constant?
    ,,   if intermitting, how often *on*, and for how long daily?
    ,,   to poorer districts, by wells, pumps, stand-pipes, butts?
    ,,   If in houses, at what charge?
    ,,   by Water Company, or in hands of local authority?

20. Early isolation of persons sick of infectious disorders?

21. Special carriages for their conveyance?

22. Public carriages prohibited from taking them under a penalty?

23. Means for disinfection { Of houses and privies?
Of sewers?
Of clothing, bedding, &c.

24. District hospitals or refuges?

25. Fever or small-pox hospitals, or wards?

26. Receiving houses for the dead?

27. Convalescent establishments, in town or country?

28. Nature and extent of lodging accommodation for the working classes?

29. Proceedings against overcrowding under Sanitary Act, 1866, or previous Acts?

30. Slaughter-houses { Public, under local authority?
Private, in what condition, and under what regulations?
Within the town?
Outside the town?

If any of my previous correspondents, or any one into whose hands this pamphlet may fall, can furnish me with additional information regarding the towns I have referred to, or others not included in my enquiries, they will confer a very great favour by filling up this schedule, or any part of it, and returning it signed, to me, at 75, Grosvenor Street, London, W.

A. P. STEWART.

LEGAL ASPECTS OF SANITARY REFORM.

BY EDWARD JENKINS, Barrister-at-Law.

Public health is public wealth. Every person laid aside by ill health is so much subtracted from the power and capacity of the State; and more than this, every person so laid aside is a drain upon the resources of the state. It takes more money to keep him than if he were well; one or more other persons in health are withdrawn from productive operations to expend their strength and time upon his recovery. If one-third of a town, or city, or state, is suffering from disease, there is cast upon the other two-thirds a proportionately greater amount of exertion than would otherwise be required of them, and there is exacted from them a proportionately greater contribution to the general expenditure, while there is less capacity both of work and contribution in the whole community. Time was when this obvious principle was unrecognised, and the state, which made paternal regulations to secure the health of men's souls—the state, which went to war to protect their liberties, and spent lives to save them—wholly avoided any observation of those permanent and subtle causes of danger to the health of the citizens that were likely to exist wherever two or three were gathered together in community of houses or homes. Even in England, where every sort of ill and grievance has been searched out with keen anxiety, while we were emancipating negroes, enfranchising householders, and abolishing oppressive taxations, the public health, a matter one would conceive of super-eminent importance, was neglected. By the course of two or three epidemics, and the philanthropic activity of a few earnest men, the public was fairly frightened into inquiry, and the result of inquiry alarmed the government into action. Since 1847, a succession of statutes has attested the importance assumed by this subject, and virtually the whole of our public health legislation is comprised within the last two decades. This legisla-

tion has worked wonders, and, with all its imperfection, was accomplished in the face of indifference and opposition, and has been impeded by the stupidity or neglect of local authorities. The government, obstructed on all hands, has been obliged to do its work in detail, and to carry measure after measure against the protest of what a recent writer on this question terms "indignant Bumbledom."

The Acts which constitute this legislation have been most various in their subjects and extent, and are enumerated in the paper of my friend, Dr. Stewart.

The compass of this legislation proves how vast and numerous were the evils to be remedied; its fragmentary character shows how gradually the public has been aroused to see the necessity of action; and it might have been supposed that after so large and apparently exhaustive a course of enactments, but little remained to be done to make the measures for the preservation of public health perfect and complete. In truth it is far otherwise. The Sanitary Act of the last session was an attempt to redress the imperfections and follies of past legislation—an attempt said to have been the result of many years' consideration—yet we think we shall be able to show that at this moment the whole of our sanitary-system is constructed upon a bad basis, and requires both amendment and consolidation.

The number and variety of Acts, of amendments to them, of bodies or persons to whom their execution is committed—the fact that in many important cases the wording of the Acts leaves a discretion as to the execution of their provisions in the local authorities, who generally are disinclined to do anything that involves an addition to the rates, are chief among many reasons for a comprehensive review and amendment. Again, there are sections in local Acts and in general Acts which are collateral, aimed at the same nuisances, but in different words, and with differing remedies. Does "The Sanitary Act of 1866," in an effectual way modify or remove the faults and deficiences of former legislation? Does it grasp the whole subject in a comprehensive way and propound a scheme which is at once feasible and complete? We think not. We think its most ardent propagators will acknowledge that it does not, and that it cannot be accepted as a piece of final legislation. It is eminently suggestive, but in many instances, as we shall see, far from efficient. It makes important advances from a sanitary point of view, but from a legal point of view it continues the errors of previous enactments. We can only hope in the few minutes allotted to us to show in a general way what we conceive to be the main faults of our present system, and we shall endeavour to refer only to those upon which there is likely to be the broadest antagonism.

The most obvious and important deficiency is the absence of a central overlooking power. The bodies appointed in different places to carry out the statutory provisions require to be placed under a capital council, committee, or ministry of public health, exercising over them a salutary supervision, and, in proper cases, endued with power to compel them in a summary manner to do their duty. This

has been objected to as a step in the direction of centralisation which would be injurious to local liberty and fraught with political danger. The distinction must, however, be remarked between *central supervision* and *central administration*. The former is compelling others to do their duty, the latter is doing duty by means of others. In the one case there is a certain amount of independence in the agents, in the latter there is none. This distinction ought to be regarded in assigning its duties to the proposed body. It should also be remembered that the administration of sanitary measures is of national as well as of local importance. Diseases amongst men and cattle, if not stayed in one district, proceed to another. The cholera at Southampton or Liverpool is an event of thrilling interest at London and Birmingham and Bristol, and, unfortunately, experience proves it to be unlikely that local authorities will have sufficient breadth either of patriotism or power to move for anything but self-preservation. Moreover, sanitary administration, to be at all effective, must be of the most summary character. The question of health or sickness to a whole district may simply be a question of hours. Should the local authority be slow in action, the machinery of the law, which works in a methodical order, may only be set in motion when it is too late to remedy the evil. Or, supposing the legal remedy to be specific and speedy—a very rare case—there may be wanting the individual who will be public-spirited enough to take the initiative against the local authority.

In proof of this, we may allude to a case brought before a branch meeting of the British Medical Association on the 26th of January last by Dr. Stewart. "In the autumn of last year he had been in a village in Hampshire in which the drainage arrangements were in the highest degree defective—the only drain being a watercourse. He had obtained the Acts with the view of aiding some of the inhabitants in an attempt to obtain improved drainage; but after reading them had been left in a state of utter confusion, and was only able to arrive at some meaning by erasing the repealed portions of the Public Health Act. Several of the inhabitants were willing to pay two-thirds, or even three-fourths, of the expense of the drainage, if the parish authorities would raise the remainder by a rate. Of this, however, there seemed no likelihood, and the principal obstruction was the surveyor. The Board of Guardians refused to act, and said that any householder might apply to the justices. He (Dr. Stewart) had consulted a high authority, and was told that a *mandamus* from the Court of Queen's Bench was the only mode of obtaining that which was desired. Rather than have recourse to this, those who were desirous of improving the sanitary condition of the place thought it might be better to carry out the drainage at their own expense."

In this instance, as Dr. Stewart has since informed us, the condition of the place, which had six hundred inhabitants, was such as to justify serious apprehensions in the event of the outbreak of an epidemic. The stench from the watercourse was at times unbearable—there

were some houses and stables round which the overflowing feculent matter of dungheaps and *cloacæ* lay in stagnant pools, not only sending up a continual miasma, but being absorbed into the walls of rooms in which human beings were living, eating, and sleeping. Had the place been within the operation of the Public Health and Local Government Acts, there would have been an effectual remedy, but before either of those Acts could be brought to bear upon the district, two-thirds of the owners and ratepayers must have agreed to it. The consequence was that this place, like a great number of large villages and towns in the kingdom, was left to the sanitary provisions of the Nuisances Removal Act of 1855, a measure which we shall presently show to be quite inadequate in the emergencies which arise.

Indeed there is a general complaint against the local authorities. To this complaint it is right to say there are some exceptions —that, for instance, of St. George's Hanover Square, to which Dr. Druitt gives a high character. The local authorities there however are selected from one of the most superior constituencies in the kingdom, and comprise men of position and wealth. St. Pancras is a more distinguished specimen on the other side. Dr. Stewart's Hampshire village is another. Mr. Jabez Hogg says of his parish, that "there is a sanitary committee which has the power of ordering improvements, unless where an expenditure of money is required, in which case the board of guardians must be consulted. He has found, as a member of the board, that the greatest obstruction to sanitary improvements came from educated men, from lawyers." The testimony of Mr. Lord of Hampstead is, "that in Hampstead, which would be supposed to be very healthy, there is much disease from time to time; but the attempts made to prevail on the board of guardians and vestry to carry out the necessary sanitary improvement, are often in vain. What is wanted, is a more coercive power over the local authorities." But the opinions of the most distinguished men are but indifferent in comparison with facts, and these of a conclusive character are readily forthcoming. The most complete sanitary legislation to be found perhaps on any Statute Book, is that relating to the metropolis. The Board of Works may be said to have had accorded to it an almost tyrannical sanitary sway, which is supplemented by powers and injunctions put upon the various vestries and district boards. Here at least we might expect to find a perfect system practically carried out. The recent epidemic has, however, proved that the immense rates imposed upon metropolitan inhabitants, and the great powers conferred upon local authorities, have not secured to London a sufficient sanitary system. Surveyors either forget or omit to do their duty, inspectors are either careless or are not numerous enough to cope with the labours requisite to so vast a field, vestries and boards are either indifferent or incapable, and perhaps even the Board of Works, while executing the great drainage schemes, has been deficient in attention to lesser details. Mr. Humphreys, the able Coroner for Middlesex, whose activity during the recent epidemic entitles him to high honour and gratitude, in a letter to *The*

Standard thus described a few places which he visited in the east end of London.

" I supply a few instances that have come under my immediate notice, even since the advent of the cholera, showing the miserable defects of water supply and drainage, the disgusting condition and arrangements of closets, the total disregard of cleanliness of houses, overcrowding, and removal of putrid vegetable and animal rubbish.

" I will take Bethnal Green.—No. 32, Chilton Street. Tenants say privy blocked up for three months ; not rectified for months after complaints made to parish authorities; no water-butts, very insufficient water supply, and that in cellars, and without drains to carry off surplus water ; there is also a collection of putrid rubbish in cellar, there being no dust-bin, and smell therefrom most offensive and dangerous ; dust very seldom removed ; house and others adjoining not whitewashed or cleaned for years.

"No. 7, Thomas Street.—One tenant states his room not white-washed or cleaned for thirty years. The collector found him white-washing it one day, and told him it would fetch a shilling a week more when done, and so he should charge him that sum, whereupon he left off, and where he left off is plainly visible.

"No. 9, Vincent Street.—Formal notice given to authorities there; the privy stopped and soaking through the floor three weeks since, not rectified on Wednesday last.

"Old Nichol Street.—Small houses ; in one forty-five people, another forty-one ; water supply (eighteen gallon cask) alongside privy and dust-bin ; no covers to water-butt or dust-bin.

" Sherwood Place.—Here is a yard at back nine feet by eleven feet for use of twenty-two people (*the property of a vestryman*); in centre is an open drain, closet flows through it, sending its stench and filth to the surface; over this open drain the inmates dry their linen ; also in this yard an open dust-hole full of decayed vegetable and animal matter ; in corner a privy without water, and adjoining it an open water-butt ; putting one's hands into the water, pressing the side, a thick, foul, and horrible slime came off, and stuck tenaciously to one's fingers.

" 31, Turvill Street.—Family of six in one small room ; entrance to yard through cellar; in yard one water pipe for three houses of thirty-seven people, and three large workshops, a very small water-butt between the drain and adjoining privy, which is without water and untrapped; large collection of putrid vegetable matter and rubbish in yard.

" I could multiply instances to any extent, both in this and other parishes, but fear to occupy too much space. Need I add that cholera and its attendant miseries reign in such localities ?"

Another letter from the Rev. Andrew A. W. Drew, incumbent of St. Michael's, Nunhead, is of yet greater significance, as it relates to dwellings recently erected, for the deficiencies of which no excuse whatever can be offered. Mr. Drew, however, appears to have mistaken the powers of the Board of Works, and to have confounded them with those of the district board. The latter, from Mr. Drew's statement, appears to have neglected or been ignorant of its duty. He says :—

"The following description of houses lately built, and others now building, will answer for itself how far the Board of Works is doing what it professes to do. In this immediate neighbourhood there exists a certain nest of cottages, which bear the most unenviable notoriety on account of being the constant possessors of small-pox, scarlet fever, and other diseases ; and to my certain knowledge there has been at least one death from cholera. A description of this nest I will endeavour to give. It consists of four parallel rows of cottages, with a fifth row running across one end of them. The other end is hemmed in by houses of a better class. In row No. 1 there are nine small cottages ; these have yards at the back about thirty-five feet long. Row No. 2 (eight cottages) faces the same way as No. 1, and is approached by a narrow mud path. Row No. 3 (eleven cottages) is placed back to back with No. 2. and each has a garden or yard, of the enormous length of twelve feet, so that the backs of the houses in these two rows are twenty-four feet apart. Row No. 4 (eleven cottages) faces No. 3, a narrow court dividing them, while Row No. 5 commands from its upper windows a bird's-eye view of all the others. From one of these windows I looked out a few days ago, and the sight I saw was quite enough to account for any amount of preventible disease. Looking down the space dividing now No. 2 from No. 3, I saw the whole of the water supply for both of them. This was contained in open cisterns, placed immediately over the out-door closets, not, however, that the closets had any benefit from the proximity of the water, but rather because they supplied a convenient resting-place for the sole receptacle for water for all purposes, drinking included. The dimensions of these cisterns were about ten feet by four and one foot deep, and one cistern supplies two houses. Every one of these cisterns was uncovered, but the surface of the water in each was covered with a thick layer of green slime (similar to that seen in stagnant ponds). I am told that this cannot be prevented from accumulating so long as the cisterns remain uncovered. The sanitary arrangements of these cottages are simply disgraceful: They are, it is true, drained, but only into a huge cesspool in one of the gardens, while there is no lack of water, as regards quantity, only of cisterns to hold it; and to crown all, the main drain of the metropolitan system runs within fifty yards of these cottages, some twenty-seven feet beneath the roadway, and yet they are as guiltless of proper drainage as if they were in Honolulu or Kaffraria. You will think this rather a bad state of things already, and that these cottages are too much crowded together ; but their owners are of another opinion. In describing row No. 1, I stated that the cottages in that row had gardens thirty-five feet long or thereabouts. This space is now being divided, and another row of cottages erected upon it. Let it be remembered that this could never take place without the consent of the Board of Works, and then let it be understood who is to blame in the matter.

The vestrymen say they can do nothing when the Board of Works has given its sanction to the erection of the cottages; that these being once passed by the surveyor of the Board, the landlords cannot be compelled to cover cisterns, lay on water to closets, or keep their property in habitable condition. I, for one, should like to know why the Board of Works ever sanctioned the erection of these cottages, and why its authorities are allowing others to be built within a few feet of them? I should like to draw their attention to the materials being used upon the new row of cottages. An inhabitant of row No. 2 pointed out to me a heap of stuff within six feet of his door, which stuff he informed me had been taken out of a cesspool. I asked what they were going to do with it, and the answer was ' make mortar of it.' Complaint was made of the stench arising from this stuff, and it was moved a little further off, but it is, I believe, still intended for mortar. Should you be able to give me a corner for this letter, I am sure the working men of this place will be deeply indebted to you, for I am writing in their interest, and making known grievances which they cannot themselves ventilate. The insertion of these particulars, which I could with ease multiply, cannot fail to point out the best cure for cholera—namely, a little energy on the part of the Board of Works in preventing the erection of fever nests and cholera traps such as abound in this place."

Yet more flagrant and startling instances are given by Dr. Fowler, in a letter to the *Times* of September 17th, which we quote at length because of its great importance :—

" Since my appointment as medical visitor about 300 houses have been inspected by my assistant and myself. These houses are tenanted by from one to ten or more families, and some of them are inhabited by nearly fifty people. My daily reports give abundant proofs of (*a*) overcrowding, and consequently filthy rooms; (*b*) filthy, defective, and inefficient privy accommodation; (*c*) foul, defective, and sometimes inefficient water supply; and (*d*) imperfect, defective, and inefficient cleansing of private and public ash-pits, and of public courts, alleys, and bye streets.

" While I candidly admit that since the third week in July much has been done in furtherance of sanitary improvement, I am compelled to announce that, at all events in Bishopsgate, much of this is more superficial than real. Courts, alleys, and houses have been lime-whited. Chloride of lime and carbolic acid have of late been our daily familiars. Nevertheless, in the ninth and tenth weeks of the present epidemic my daily inspections continue to reveal the innate horrors of cholera nests.

" Catherine-wheel Alley leads directly from the main thoroughfare into Petticoat Lane. Scarcely a day has passed without my forwarding a description of this foul place. Pass down it when you will, eyes and nose will be assailed with the sight and stink of scattered heaps of every disgusting species of organic filth. This condition evidently in part arises from the fact that Nos. 4, 5, 6, and 7, Cock Hill, have no dust-bin. The refuse caused by the twenty-eight persons in these houses is daily thrown into this adjacent alley. At No. 23 in this said alley, on the 28th of July, occurred the first two (and fatal) cases of cholera among Bishopsgate residents. In eight small rooms reside twenty-nine people. The house has no dustbin. On the 15th and 17th of September the condition of its sole privy was most disgusting. It had no water supply. The pan was overflowingly full, the contents, indeed, covered seat and flooring both. These lethal matters were also scattered all over the otherwise sufficiently filthy yard, and even on the different floors of the rooms. The house was, indeed, a most fit palace for the goddess Cloacina. From the cellar of No. 21 the seventeen inhabitants of the house are daily regaled with the fumes arising from the cleaning and preparing of cowheels and tripe. On September 15, at No. 28, lived twenty-four people in six rooms, one of which, on the second floor, was apparently the sole bed-room for eleven human beings. The one privy of this house was in a similar state to the one above described. It had no water supply ; neither was there, nor had there been for some time, a single drop of water for the other wants of these two dozen poor. Need I say that I have cases of diarrhœa in almost every house in this alley?

" A similar condition of things obtains in the adjoining cholera and diarrhœa nests—Windsor and Sandy Streets.

" On the 10th of September, at No. 10 in the former, resided nineteen people, and their one privy was unsupplied with water, and so on at No. 9 with its twenty-five tenants, Nos. 11, 13, 8, with its twenty tenants, and No. 2. The same votive offerings to Cloacina were here and there conspicuously present, especially in the privies and yards of Nos. 9 and 13. From these several houses the dust had not been removed for weeks. On the 17th of September these disgusting details were still unrectified. On the 4th of September, at No. 5, Sandy Street, there was only one filthy privy, out of repair, for the use of forty-seven people. On the 11th of September there was neither any water supply nor any privy at all for the accommodation of the fifteen inhabitants of No. 3, Montague Court. In the fifteen houses of this court lived 152 people, and most, if not all, of the privies, were unsupplied with water, were filthy, and were covered with human excreta. In two of these houses girls of fourteen and fifteen were ascertained to sleep in the same bed with their fathers.

" On September 13, at No. 1, Swan Yard, which is a large mews and depôt for carrier's carts, there resided over the several stables fifty-six people, besides the dogs and cats. The six families of twenty-eight people were allotted one waterless privy and one water-tank ; to eight other families of twenty-four people were allotted one other privy and one water-tank. The whole yard was in a beastly state. Pools of liquid manure were running from the several dungheaps to amalgamate with a mass of filth in the centre of the yard. One of the dungheaps had not been emptied for three or four weeks, and adjoining thereto was a stinking public privy. The water-tank, which was said to supply only the horses, was uncovered and full of animalculæ and vegetable organisms. On September 17, a case of cholera was taken from one of these rooms to the temporary Cholera Hospital in New Street.

" Lamb Alley passes from alongside my house behind the right-hand side of Sun Street. Each day finds its gully-holes and gutters blocked up and reeking with semi-liquid, stinking filth. At No. 3 in this said alley lived, on September 10th, seventeen people, without any water supply or privy accommodation. In six of the houses in Blyth's Buildings (which form a hollow square opening into this alley) resided, on September 10th, seventy-eight people, for whose use there were only two filthy waterless privies. In Clement's Place, another blind offshoot from Lamb Alley, resided, on the same day, in eight small houses, nearly 100 people.

" At No. 6, one room 11 feet by $7\frac{1}{2}$ feet, was the dormitory for three adults and five children. Most of the privies in this place had no water. Two cases of cholera, each fatal in less than twenty hours, were furnished last week from one of these tenements. On the 1st of September, at 65, Sun Street (fronting Lamb Alley), both diarrhœa and small pox were in the house, which literally stunk of sewer gas emanating from the one privy, which, with the uncovered and uncleansed water-butt and house refuse, was in the cellar and practically useless. It was in such a filthy, water-less state, with the old excrement welling up and filling the pan, that no one of the nineteen inhabitants had been able to avail themselves of it for some considerable time. On the 14th of September this house was in the same state. No attention to or alteration of these disgusting matters had been paid or effected.

" Such are some few instances of the present flagrant condition of affairs in my district.

" A retrospect of my earlier inspections would furnish numerous similar details. Day after day have I transmitted the result of my own and my assistant's inquiries to the deputed receiver of these reports. By section 6 of the aforesaid Order of Council it is the duty of the Board of Guardians to, without delay, cause a report of such facts to be made to the nuisances removal authority—i.e., the Commissioners of City Sewers. Some half-dozen repetitions have I in as many weeks sent in of some of the above statements. My very first report was of the filthy and overcrowded condition of No. 140, Bishopsgate Street Without. Although I then stated that ' This house requires the constant supervision of an inspector of nuisances,' its state on the 15th inst. was in the main no better than it was six weeks ago when visited with cholera.

" Although west of the boundary line of the field of the East London Waterworks' mains, the sub-district of St. Botolph, East London district, has (as has been authoritatively stated) suffered severely from the present visitation. During the last week four deaths out of five admissions occurred in the temporary cholera hospital in New Street. There was, indeed, a sudden outburst of fatal cholera in Bishopsgate parish.

" The facts I have delineated perhaps explain this. At all events, they sufficiently show the palpable absurdity of drenching our streets with carbolic acid, and of even lime-whiting the interior of houses, while blots far deeper and more foul are left to poison the physical and moral humanity of our poor."

The medical profession throughout the country concur in the opinion that the local authorities generally need to be overlooked. Dr. Druitt suggests that their powers should be enlarged, but the opinion of his medical brethren is against him. " Is it not a fact," says a writer in the *British Medical Journal*, " that in many places the local authorities are the systematic and bitter opponents of sanitary reform ? We are anxious to ascertain in how many instances the wise and beneficent intentions of the legislature are defeated by the passive resistance or dogged opposition of the local authorities, who will not avail themselves of the ample permissive powers which the law gives them ; and whether the time has not come when, in the interest of the public, the discharge of duties which is now optional should not be made compulsory—whether in short there should not be some court of last resort, to which the enlightened few may appeal for speedy justice from the ignorance, prejudice or parsimony of the local authorities." The 49th section of the " Sanitary Act" endeavours to provide a remedy for the difficulty to which we have just adverted, and to establish a sort of court of speedy resort in cases of default on the part of local authorities. Should a sewer authority make default in providing its district with sufficient sewers, or in maintaining its sewers, or in supplying water, or should a nuisance authority " make default in enforcing the provisions of the Nuisance Removal Act, &c., complaint may be made to a Secretary of State, who, after due inquiry, may make an order limiting a time for the performance of its duty in the matter of such complaint." The inconvenience of these applications to, and inquiries by Secretaries of State, on subjects quite foreign to their usual duties, and for the due prosecution of which no proper machinery is ready, need hardly be pointed out. If such powers may be intrusted to *them* they may more safely, as well as efficiently, be conveyed to a body selected and endowed with a special organisation for the purpose. Moreover, if the provisions of the Acts are permissive merely, there can be, since the cases will be cases of discretion, no legal " default in enforcing those provisions " which is cognisable by a Secretary of State. The new Act, for instance, enacts that it shall be lawful for nuisance authorities to provide carriages for the conveyance of infected persons, and that the sewer authority may provide district hospitals ; it cannot for a moment be supposed that these or any other merely suggestive provisions come within the scope of the 49th section to which we have alluded. The word " duty" implies something which has been enjoined, and not something which has only been suggested.

We may now shortly state who the authorities are. They are differently constituted in the City of London, in the metropolitan districts, in places under the Local Government Act, and in other places throughout the country. In London the commissioners of sewers are the local authority for carrying out sanitary measures under the City Sewers Act. In the rest of the metropolis, the vestries of the parishes or the district boards formed under the Metropolis Management Acts, are the local authorities. In places under the Public Health and Local Government Acts, the Board of Health for the place, that is, in corporate towns the council, and in other places the town improvement commissioners or an elective board is the local authority. It ought to be observed that the Nuisances Removal Acts operate collaterally or cumulatively with the Metropolis Management and other Local Government Acts, and that there may be found instances of two different enactments applicable to the same cases, with differing penalties for the same offences. Elsewhere, under the Nuisances Removal Acts, the local authority consists of the mayor, aldermen, and burgesses by the council, where a council exists: where there are trustees or commissioners under an Improvement Act, such trustees or commissioners; where none of these, the board of guardians of the poor; and if no such board, the overseers of the poor for the place or parish.

We have thus particularly described the local authorities because of their variety, and we shall hereafter have occasion to mark, that various as they are, they have not had entrusted to them all the details of sanitary administration; a fact from which, as may readily be supposed, no little complication arises.

Properly speaking, however, and generally the real local authority before and we suppose since the recent Act, has been a sanitary committee appointed by the various bodies for the purpose of enforcing the "Nuisances Removal," the "Diseases Prevention," and now the "Sanitary" Acts. The sanitary provisions of other Acts do not ordinarily come within the scope of this committee's powers, and cases under them are referred to the vestry, "which," says Dr. Druitt, "is sure to be a larger, more divided, and less manageable body than the smaller committee which constitutes the usual local authority."

When we come to examine the machinery by which these bodies are to perform their duties, we light upon a curious anomaly. In the metropolis, the local authority *is obliged* to appoint medical officers of health and inspectors of nuisances, but under the Public Health and Local Government Acts the appointment of a medical officer is optional, that of an inspector necessary, while in all other places, with but few exceptions, there is no obligation on the local authority to employ either.

This anomaly is the result of retrograde legislation. Under the Nuisances Removal Act of 1855, the local authority was bound to employ or join with other local authorities in employing a sanitary inspector or inspectors. The Amendment Act of 1860 repealed this provision, and substituted a permission to the guardians of any union or parish not within an union to employ one of their medical officers to report upon the sanitary state of the union or parish. How this permission has been accepted and taken advantage of by the authorities, we may judge from the important statistics collected by the energy of Dr. Stewart. From these we can form an idea of the nature of that supervision under which a large number of towns existed at a time when the kingdom was exposed to an outbreak of cholera. From these it is not too wide an inference to draw, that two-thirds of England is practically destitute of sanitary control. The importance of this point was earnestly brought to the attention of the government when the Public Health Bill was in committee, but it received no solution at their hands.

We hardly think it necessary to urge, with any lergthened argument, that the power to appoint medical officers, analysts, and inspectors of nuisances ought to be exercised throughout the kingdom. Where the appointment of any of these has been compulsory, as in the metropolis, the valuable services they have rendered the public by bringing scientific knowledge and practical experience to bear upon the multitudinous nuisances of collected population cannot be estimated. Private persons will endure a great deal before they will engage in anything involving expense. To look after these people when they are themselves in fault, or to lend a ready ear to their complaints when they are aggrieved by others, to scent out nuisances and abolish them, is the business of officers and inspectors, and no corner of the country should be unknown to their supervision.

But we have seen that even where these officers have been appointed, they may yet have to contend against the ignorance and stupidity of local authorities. The renowned instance of St. Pancras proves that vestries and boards, composed of tradesmen, or licensed victuallers, or small householders and the like, are not open to the warnings and suggestions of capable officers. The value of a proposition is by them likely to be estimated in the inverse ratio of the demand it involves upon the rates. Under these circumstances, it is essential that the officer should be independent of the local authority. There is less danger in his independence, because he only suggests and reports ; but if his appointment is at the will of the local authority, he may be simply their creature, or if not their creature, may suffer from the displeasure with which they view his sanitary activity. The appointment and removal of every local inspector and medical officer should therefore be subject to the approval of a central authority, which is itself responsible to Parliament.

The oversight of the medical officers is, however, but a slight part of that sanitary system, at the head of which we desire to place a ministry or board of health. There is the more extended and important oversight of localities and local authorities. The complaint now is, that unless the statutes specifically ordain that certain things shall be done, the authorities will not do them. Very often the statutes give an uncertain sound, and persons who wish to have a judicial exposition of them must resort to the expensive machinery of the law. The law, in too many cases guided more by the letter than the spirit, refuses to enlarge the meaning of Acts which involve personal rights, and presents the man who appeals against the sanitary inactivity of a board or vestry with a logical reason for the perpetuity of a nuisance. Two things, therefore, require to be done. *The provisions of the statutes should be enacted plainly and imperatively, and the central authority should employ national inspectors to watch the sanitary condition of the kingdom, to suggest improvements, to report and investigate complaints.*

A few instances will prove the first necessity. The want of plainness in the wording of the Acts often leads to serious perplexity. The metropolitan officers give an example in their " Suggestions." " Section 8 and section 27 of the Nuisances Removal Act (1855) have practically been found to clash. If, in a case of nuisance, *e.g.* offensive odours, arising from a trade accumulation, substances used in a business, &c., a summons be taken out under section 27, it is pleaded that the summons should have been taken out under section 8. On taking one out under section 8, an order is objected to, on the ground that the means adopted are sufficient for the protection of public health, or that the deposit was not kept longer than the defendant required it for the purposes of his business. The latter excuse can never be got over. As to the former, it has to be proved that what causes offensive odour also damages health, and in many cases of offensive accumulations this cannot be maintained in the present state of our knowledge. Again, if an order should by any chance be obtainable, and the accumulation be removed, the offensive matters may be immediately replaced, and being newly deposited, must remain again, so long as the manufacturer has need for them in his business." Again, under section 21 of the Nuisances Removal Act 1855, where ditches are foul or offensive, there is *a discretion* left in the surveyor as to cleansing them.

Under section 22, " Whenever any ditch, &c., used, or partly used, for the conveyance of any water, filth, sewage, or other matter from any house, &c., is a nuisance within the meaning of the Act, and cannot, *in the opinion of the local authority*, be rendered innocuous, without the laying down of a sewer, or some other structure, &c., they shall, and are thereby required", to make and keep it in repair. But by the words italicised, absolute discretion is left to the authorities, for no court would inquire into the reasonableness of the " opinion of the local authority," although the succeeding words are strongly imperative. In none of these instances has the new Act afforded any relief. The manufacturers may still baffle the local authorities by their difficult dilemma, the surveyor and local authorities retain their discretion. It is true, that the 20th section of the Act enacts that "it shall be the duty of the nuisance authority to make, from time to time, either by itself, or its officers, inspection of the district, with a view to ascertain what nuisances exist, calling for abatement under the powers of the Nuisance Removal Acts, and *to enforce the provisions of the said Acts*, in order to cause the abatement thereof." But we have shown " the provisions of the said Acts" to be inadequate, making it optional with the surveyor to clean, and with the local authority to do structural works, and as it is those provisions which are to be enforced, the new enactment would not, in these instances at least, produce any legal difference.

Let us take another case. The 16th section of the Nuisances Removal Act enacts that when "it shall appear to the justices that the execution of structural works is required for the abatement of a nuisance they may direct such works to be carried out." A case in which the abatement of a nuisance depended upon structural works would be one of strong necessity, yet the Court of Queen's Bench has decided that such an enactment is only permissive, and the justices cannot be compelled by mandamus to direct the works to be done.*

The "Sanitary Act, 1866," is in many of its new and most important particulars permissive. We cannot doubt the intentions of the government in urging its adoption upon Parliament with some earnestness. The threatened invasion of cholera enabled them to exercise a pressure which was judicious, if the Act be considered as a merely temporary enactment, but not so if it should be permanent. It was felt and said at the time of its passage by members of the government that further consolidation and revision were required. We have endeavoured to show what direction any new legislation should take. To a sanitary reformer there is no greater bugbear than a permissive enactment. A suggestion which involves expense to persons interested in that expense is sure, in nine cases out of ten, to be unheeded. We have not far to search in the late Act for such suggestions. The 10th section provides that, " If a dwelling-house within the district of a sewer authority is without a drain, or without such drain as is sufficient for effectual drainage," two cases of vital importance, the sewer authority *may* require the owner to make a drain emptying into one of their sewers ; or if no such means of drainage are within a specified distance, then emptying into such covered cesspool or other place, not being under any house, as the sewer authority directs, &c." We have been unable to discover a reason why this should not have been mandatory. If no sewer runs within a practicable distance of a house, the only alternative must be to make a proper cesspool. Why should not the nuisance authority be compelled to see that the house is made habitable by one or the other method? So, as we have already seen, the provision of means of disinfection, of sick carriages, of places for the reception of dead bodies, of sick hospitals, is left to the option of the authorities. Let any one look over the lists, prepared by Dr. Stewart, of the appointment of medical officers, and judge whether it is probable that these latter suggestions will be received and acted upon.

The appointment of national inspectors to act under the central authority, seems necessarily to follow from the existence of that authority. Wide as its powers might be, its presence and observation

---

* *In re* The Local Board of Health of the parish of Ham, 7 E. & B. 280. 26 L. J. M. C. 43.

could not be everywhere. It would need agents, like those able men who have been employed with such great success by the Privy Council on many occasions—to examine into and report upon complaints (which, under certain restrictions, ought to be easily and inexpensively received)—to suggest and overlook improvements—to investigate causes of disease—whose duty, in fact, it should be to watch the sanitary condition of the whole kingdom. These inspectors, uninfluenced by local prejudices, would be able to return impartial reports upon the action of local authorities and the needs of places. Through them, when there was a conflict of interests, the committee could justly balance the obligations of those interests. This machinery would be simple and comparatively uncostly, and the courts would be relieved of a great burden.

We have now approached in contemplation something like a system. A central authority, with a staff of officers, overseeing and directing local authorities with their officers. But supposing this to be constituted, there would still remain to be remedied the deficiencies and inefficiencies of the laws which this organisation was to put in execution. Some of these we have designated, others we are obliged for the present to avoid. Many have been ably pointed out by Mr. Rumsey in the *Journal of Social Science* for October, 1866. The exclusion of clergymen from participation in sanitary management, the intrusion into sanitary boards of members of water and gas companies, whose interests are naturally opposed to those of the ratepayers, are matters that require redress. More important is the question, whether the supply of water and gas by private companies should not be forbidden, and the consumers be also the makers. This question should be discussed by itself, and perhaps at no distant day we may have it properly treated by some competent member of this Association. But one obvious deficiency we think it needful to mention. All sanitary matters should come within the management of one authority. In administration of laws human, unlike laws divine, "diversities of operations" are obstructive. The common lodging houses Acts are not carried out by the local authority, but by police magistrates and justices. The local authority for the appointment of analysts out of the metropolis, is the court of quarter sessions of every county, and the town council of every borough having a separate jurisdiction.

Such appear to us to be the main faults and needed improvements in our public health laws. With compulsory enactments, and an efficient ministry or board of health, we might see some prospect of the sanitary regeneration of the country. Two things, let us again urge, concur to enforce upon us the necessity of the proposed supervision, namely, the indifference of private persons to sanitary precautions, and the inefficiency of the bodies whose duty it is to watch the public health. The former of these causes will exhibit itself even in cases where only a little personal attention is needed in the pursuit of relief ; while that uncertain and expensive machinery of the law, whether in inferior or superior courts, to which we have alluded, and from which all men naturally shrink, is not always ductile. Its motions are subject to fixed rules; its instructions are settled and precise, leaving no discretion; it is constrained by the inflexibility of words, and drilled into the regiments of logic. The judge dare not ignore the language in extracting the spirit; he dare not stretch his power beyond the dimensions of his office, which is to declare, and not to make the law. Often, therefore, when the whole moral force of an enactment, and of judicial conviction, and of popular opinion, is against some act or thing, that act or thing may exist and be done in spite of all, because it is impossible for the most keen-eyed legislator to forecast every contingency in a world of perpetually-varying combinations, and to prescribe in distinct terms the remedies or penalties for every evil that might naturally be included within the sphere of a law. In most cases that come within the province of legislation it is not of so much consequence that the law should be summary as that it should be sure. The march of criminal justice, and the settlement of civil rights, acquire both certainty and dignity from the deliberation of their process. But there are cases where the benefit of the body social demands a flexible jurisdiction and a summary proceeding—demands even a little temporary or individual injustice for the lasting good of a great number.· Some such jurisdiction and process might, perhaps, with great industry and much parliamentary wrangling, be devised for the sanitary security of the kingdom. It might be possible to construct a series of regulations so numerous and so minute that but few and rare instances of ineffectual powers or remedies could occur. Yet there would still stand and face us the two cardinal difficulties—INDIFFERENCE and EXPENSE. The very minuteness and delicacy of our instrument would make men shrink from using it—would be likely to bring about the complication which increases costs. The very summariness which is proved to be essential to the practicability of a sanitary system, would make the judges cautious in their interpretation, the justices hesitating in their orders. To define, therefore, peremptorily the most obvious and important duties of the local authorities,—to give them a fair opportunity of voluntarily pursuing them,—to place over them a body whose office it shall be, not to regulate their actions, but to redress their errors and omissions, and to prosecute at the public, and not at individual expense, those who disobey sanitary enactments,—to give this body a wide discretion with reference to the thousand matters and things relating to public health which legislation cannot provide against,—are the propositions which we now press upon Parliament as the result of our inquiry and argument. The imperfection of the present laws in themselves, and the inadequacy of their practical enforcement, will, during the meeting of this Congress, be sufficiently evidenced. It is needless to appeal to sentiments of fear, of self-preservation. It cannot now be required to be shown that the best preventive of epidemic disorders is constant sanitary vigilance, or even that the truest economy is that which, by a moderate expenditure, reduces the probabilities of disease to a minimum, not that which neglects until the fatal hour the measures of precaution, and wastes a lavish sum upon means of cure. We cannot touch upon the relations of this subject to the moral improvement of the people. Wretched houses make wretched homes; and while immoral or slatternly habits convert fine dwellings into styes, it is almost as true that dirty and unhealthy habitations transfer a taint to the character and habits of the persons who occupy them. The depressing influences of filth and disease write their evidences on men's manners as well as on their skins; and if the body social and politic is to be sound, the body physical must be healthy too.

On the 2nd of April, a Deputation from the National Association for the Promotion of Social Science waited on, and submitted to, the DUKE OF MARLBOROUGH, President of the Privy Council, the following Memorial:—

The Council of the National Association for the Promotion of Social Science desires to submit to your Grace the following considerations respecting an amendment and consolidation of the laws relating to Public Health.

These laws are numerous and diverse; and, as different subjects of legislative interference arise from year to year, become more complex and more difficult to interpret and apply.

Some of the enactments are general, some local. The provisions of the latter are often of universal value and applicability, and might beneficially be introduced into the former. In other instances there are different enactments relating to the same cases, with different penalties for the same offences. For instance, section 63 of "The Public Health Act, 1848," and section 2 of "The Nuisances Removal Amendment Act," 26 and 27 Vict., c. 117, intended to prevent the sale of diseased meat, and collateral in their operation, impose a penalty; the one of £10, the other of £20, in precisely similar cases. This, of necessity, leads to confusion.

Some important enactments are permissive; indeed this principle very extensively pervades sanitary acts of the greatest importance, and consequently they are seldom acted upon. For instance, section 22 of "The Nuisances Removal Act, 1855," where, when ditches, etc., are a nuisance, it is left to "the opinion of the local authority" to decide whether the nuisance requires a sewer for its abatement; and sections 23 and 24 of "The Sanitary Act, 1866," relating respectively to the provision of means for disinfection, and of carriages for the conveyance of persons sick of infectious disorders; section 27 of the same Act and section 81 of "The Public Health Act, 1848," concerning the establish'ment of places for the reception of dead bodies; and section 52 of "The Public Health Act, 1848," with reference to compelling a proper provision of closets in factories, are all permissive.

The bodies appointed to administer health laws are not always identical, as it is evidently expedient that they should be. There are natural connections which ought not to be disregarded—e.g., the supply of water with the removal of waste; the large with the small means of drainage. These are under diverse authorities. Without bodies of more general and uniform powers, wider districts, and highly qualified officers of health precluded from private practice, health laws cannot be made fully successful in their operation. "The Sanitary Act, 1866," constitutes sewer authorities, differing, in some respects, from local authorities under other statutes. The Common Lodging

Houses Acts are committed to the management of the police in the metropolis, to Local Boards of Health, to Town Commissioners and Justices in other places. The appointment of analysts rests with the Court of Quarter Sessions in counties, and with the Town Council in boroughs having a separate peace jurisdiction, instead of with the usual authorities for sanitary purposes. Further, this most important appointment is seldom made, as the law merely gives a permission to appoint.

The local authorities are more or less unlearned, and for that reason require plain and specific directions. They are interested in diminishing the rates, unmindful of the probable costliness of their parsimony; and they are, therefore, frequently unwilling to act in sanitary matters, except under compulsion. They are often ignorant of the importance of sanitary precautions, and indifferent to flagrant nuisances, and to the serious consequences arising therefrom to individuals, to others beyond the offending district, and to society at large. Hence the need of a special and central department to stimulate an unwilling or inefficient local authority, to act as a Court of Appeal, to diffuse to all the knowledge obtained from districts that have no connection with each other, to protect individuals and minorities against injustice, and, being possessed of the highest practical knowledge, to construct or sanction bye-laws and local regulations.

The Building Acts, which should at least contain sound rules for insuring due attention to health in the erection of habitations, are very deficient indeed in this point of primary importance. In some few places bye-laws are even now made to serve the purpose. It is undeniable that without some very uniform and stringent additions and alterations to Building Acts (such as that which is now being promoted by the Metropolitan Board of Works), the construction of healthy dwellings, especially for the poorer classes, acknowledged to be required on a very large scale indeed, will most deplorably fail; and the new tenements will doubtless be as bad as the old, or even worse.

The sale of unwholesome and adulterated food calls for very serious attention, and for a much more efficient law. The present law is full of difficulties and defects, is much complained of, and is almost inoperative.

While, therefore, the Acts remain so complicated and multifarious, as are those now in force, it is impossible to hope for an efficient sanitary administration; especially as the principles underlying all true sanitary law are the same, more or less applicable in the same way in all places.

On these grounds the Council earnestly submit, for the favourable consideration of the Government—

1. That the laws of public health require to be revised and consolidated with plain and specific enactments on sanitary matters.

2. That permissive enactments are generally taken to be permissions not to act, and that therefore the most useful provisions should be made peremptory.

3. That the constitution of sanitary authorities should be more uniform; their areas of administration more extensive; their powers and functions more comprehensive; and that some provision be made for the addition of members possessing other and higher qualifications than those now required.

4. That the inefficiency in the administration of the health laws by the local authorities is in part due to the absence of a central power, which could be appealed to without reference to the courts of law, and could by means of judicious advice, and, if necessary, by legal compulsion, cause the local authorities to do their duty.

At the close of the interview, his Grace, declaring his acquiescence in the general tenour of the memorial, expressed a wish to have submitted to him in writing, or print, an epitome of the observations which had fallen from the various speakers. In accordance with this wish the following abstract of what was said has been prepared :—

Mr. RENDLE, as one of the secretaries of the Health Department of the Association, in presenting the memorial, acknowledged the great progress already made in health legislation ; but he said that it had up to this time been mainly for special cases and piecemeal, and that hence sanitary legislation had become in some instances contradictory—that various parts of it were out of harmony with each other—sometimes the same provision, with or without difference, being repeated—that much was permissive, which should be obligatory, and as a result there was confusion, with much waste of force, and discouragement in carrying out the Acts. The bodies appointed to carry out were often diverse, occasionally opposed to and hindering one another, and generally more or less unlearned, and requiring clear and specific Acts for their guidance. The great objections now hindering the due carrying out of the Sanitary Acts would for the most part be removed with a better organisation. He instanced the difficulties experienced by boards wishing to carry out the law, and handed in a statement from Chelsea to this effect, which he said was a statement which might be made by almost all other bodies desirous of working the sanitary laws. He pointed out the need of a better provision as to magistrates, the police magistrates having too much to do of a kind very little in harmony with true sanitary legislation, and, consequently, almost generally failing to help willing local authorities by their judgments. The Building Acts were almost without provisions under which healthy habitations might be erected for the poorer people in case unfit places were pulled down under any Artizans' Dwellings Bill, and he gave instances where new dwellings of this class, built, as they usually were, by poor speculative builders, very speedily became as bad or worse in their unhealthy conditions as any of the oldest. The Vaccination Acts were objectionable, because they had always been administered by the Poor Law authorities. People were taught to avoid poor-law help, and this feeling had seriously impeded vaccination, the vaccinators for a neighbourhood being too usually the poor-law surgeons only. Vaccination, of course, did not commend itself to the class of people a little above the poorest. The officer vaccinating certainly should not certify to the success of his own operation. It required a more liberal pay, an inspector who should certify and not vaccinate, and who should care for the lymph and certify as to its fitness for use. The Adulteration of Food Act, he said, was also a failure, and the poorer buyers were not protected. All that he had said by no means exhausted the catalogue of evils in the present sanitary laws of the country.

Mr. RUMSEY urged the necessity for the union and consolidation of the central authorities in sanitary matters, which are at present distributed between the Privy Council, the Home Office, the Poor Law Board, and the Registrar-General, producing uncertainty and confusion in local administration. He also pointed out the great anomalies which mark local administration in the provinces, the variety of boards existing under poor-law and local government and Public Health Acts ; and the remarkable difference in the area and population of the districts under these several boards, the inhabitants of a district varying from less than a hundred to many thousands. He recommended an improved constitution of local boards with higher qualifications for their members and the extension of areas of local government, so as to provide for an economical and efficient administration of the health laws. He showed how this extension of area affected the appointment of health officers, and urged the necessity for an entirely different system of those appointments which in the provinces were made under the Public Health Acts. He instanced the inspection of factories and work places, especially the extension of the Factory Acts now before the House of Commons, as a reason for appointing a highly-qualified class of officers rendered independent of private practice and debarred from it. He noticed the importance of such independence as regards certificates of health, age, and fitness for labour of the children employed. He also mentioned Mr. Torrens's Bill for dwellings for the labouring classes as requiring the action of a health officer, who ought certainly to be independent of the proprietors and householders of the wretched hovels he might have to condemn. The basis of an improved organisation, he considered, was to be found in the registration division of the country which are identical with the poor-law unions. It is in these districts that the great facts of disease and mortality are recorded ; in these, therefore, a scientific officer is especially needed, both to correct and verify those returns, and to apply them to the suggestion of practical remedies. It would be a most false step in sanitary legislation to compel every small local board to appoint its own officer of health on its own terms. He warned the Government against enforcing, or even encouraging the present defective system of these appointments, and urged the importance of making a new organisation of scientific persons the foundation of a truer sanitary reform.

Dr. LANKESTER said he wished generally to confirm the views expressed by Mr. Rendle. He had taken an interest for the last twenty-five years is sanitary legislation. The great defect in this legislation was its permissive character. Those to whom power was given to act for the benefit of others, might refuse to act for the benefit of their fellow citizens, and there was no power above them to compel their action. He had thus seen successive Acts of Parliament become dead letters in spite of all powers the state had given. What every one wanted who had an interest in the sanitary welfare of their fellow citizens, was some definite law on which they could act. The present position of our legislation was that local boards and authorities, might, if they thought fit, prevent disease and death, but if they did not think fit to do so there was no superior authority to compel them. The deputation was anxious to impress upon the Government the necessity for the consolidation of the present Acts of Parliament, and for placing in the hands of the central authority a power of seeing that they were carried into effect. At the present time various bodies had some kind of control in relation to sanitary legislation. The Privy Council, over whom his Grace presided, had authority in certain things, but this power was limited. By the Act of 1866, the Home Secretary was invested with power, but which at present had exerted little or no effect. Then there was the Poor Law Board, which represents the Boards of Guardians, and gives them the power of supervising vaccination and its practice throughout the country. To show the utter powerlessness of this authority to deal with the subject, it was only necessary to say that upwards of 2,000 persons had died of smallpox in England and Wales during the year 1866. Then, with regard to the supervision of lodging-houses, and the condition of houses, the Chief Commissioner of Police had power to act. Powers of other kinds were given to other bodies, and it was a most difficult thing for an officer of health, in the parishes of London, to know to what authority he was to look to to abate or prevent nuisances injurious to health. What was wanted was a unification of the laws in relation to public health, and a department of the Government having power to act in individual cases. Such a body constituted by Government should have power to compel vestries to do certain things which were obviously necessary for securing the public health. He saw with great pleasure that Mr. Rumsey was present in the deputation, as he had written one of the best books in the English language on the subject of State Medicine, and he knew no one who was more entitled to be listened to by statesmen of the present day than Mr. Rumsey.

Mr. JAMES BEAL urged the necessity for some measure of revision and consolidation. The permissive character of the present enactments was a mere loophole by which to avert responsibility. The provision of carriages for the removal of the sick of infectious diseases, and proper hospital accommodation for such cases, was avoided in this way, either to save the expense altogether, or to shift it on to other shoulders. Suggestions emanating from the district officers seldom or ever received proper consideration, and of course were as seldom acted up to. Conflicting interests would often prevent the carrying out of orders already made. The analysation of food or gas may be ordered, but a dead lock came when the expenses of providing apparatus for working it were to be provided. He complained that whilst last session the Sanitary Act of 1866 imposed upon the vestries the duty of providing hospitals for infectious diseases, this year the Poor Law Board had passed through the House, apparently without any concert with the Board of Health, a Bill imposing similar duties on Boards of Guardians. What was wanted was enlarged areas of administration for local purposes, and one central board for all London, armed with sufficient powers to enforce the action Parliament desired. The conflicting action of departments of Government was a fruitful source of weakness. Let London be placed under one Board of State, Poor Law if they liked, or Home Office, or Privy .Council, but not all three, and let the action of the State be simply appellate. He suggested that all the Health Bills and Vaccination Acts should be referred to a draughtsman to consolidate, and so end the chaotic legislation in which they were helplessly involved. He instanced regulations approved by Mr. Secretary Walpole under the Sanitary Act, 1866, for Chelsea ; precisely the same were disapproved by the same officer of State for St. James's.

Dr. STEWART drew attention to the want of carriages for the conveyance of persons ill of infectious disorders, and of any effective means for disinfection, and for the isolation of the sick in most of the large towns throughout the country. He also insisted strongly on the absence in many places of officers of health and inspectors of nuisances, to whom was committed the duty of enforcing the act for the seizure of unwholesome articles of food. In London alone was the appointment of officers of health imperative, and he showed that the size and population of their districts varied enormously, as also their salaries, one having as little as twelve guineas, another as much as £1,000 a year. Only in nineteen out of fifty-nine large districts were health officers appointed, and the average of inspection was in London one to 34,000, and in provincial towns one to 42,000, of a population, rendering impossible any effectual inspection or removal of nuisances. And, as if to complicate matters still more, and to prevent any hearty co-operation in carrying out sanitary improvements, the inspectors of nuisances were in not a few instances independent of the officer of health, under whose control they should always be placed.